£1.20

Flying Fever

AIR VICE-MARSHAL S. F. VINCENT
C.B., D.F.C., A.F.C., D.L.

Flying Fever

Foreword by
Admiral of the Fleet
The Earl Mountbatten of Burma
K.G., P.C., G.C.B., O.M.

JARROLDS, LONDON

JARROLDS PUBLISHERS (LONDON) LTD
3 Fitzroy Square, London W1

AN IMPRINT OF THE HUTCHINSON GROUP

London Melbourne Sydney Auckland
Wellington Johannesburg Cape Town
and agencies throughout the world

First published 1972

This book has been set in Times type, printed in Great Britain on antique wove paper by Anchor Press, Tiptree, Essex and bound by Leighton-Straker Bookbinding Co. Ltd., London

ISBN 0 09 112720 3

To my wife
who has been separated from me for so many
years while I flew around and about
the world.

Author's Note

I was asked to write this book which was meant to be about my flying experiences because I have always loved flying and have flown many different types of aircraft.

I have avoided, as much as possible, such remarks as 'Then I went up in a "So-and-So" and did a loop and a roll' as that would, all too quickly, have become very boring. I have, of course, had to be on the ground and even chairborne for parts of the book. I have not set out to show who did, or did not, win either war by his brilliance or stupidity. I was fortunate in being in the Royal Flying Corps and Royal Air Force and, therefore, seeing a great deal of the world and meeting many interesting people. I hope readers will get some enjoyment in sharing my experiences.

My gratitude goes to my one-time 'Supremo' in Burma, Earl Mountbatten, for writing the foreword and to Norah Lofts for her help and support. Bruce Robertson has been of great assistance in checking the script. While doing so, he crossed many Ts and dotted many Is and I am very grateful to him also.

Contents

Illustrations

Between pages 96 and 97

In the text

Foreword

by Admiral of the Fleet

The Earl Mountbatten of Burma

K.G., P.C., G.C.B., O.M.

I am glad to have been given the opportunity of writing a foreword to this book which gives such a splendid account of the life of a very active airman throughout his long and distinguished career.

I am specially glad of the opportunity of paying a heartfelt tribute to Air Vice-Marshal Stanley Vincent and to No. 221 Group, R.A.F., which he commanded throughout our victorious advance in the recovery and liberation of Burma. Indeed I am grateful not only to this Group but also to all the other Groups and formations of the air forces which I had the honour to have under my supreme command throughout the campaign.

Never have the land forces in any campaign owed more to their associated air forces for without them the army could never have carried out their victorious advance from north to south in Burma. The Japanese had advanced the easy way from the port of Rangoon in the south up the axis of river, road and rail communications. After our amphibious forces had been recalled to help with the invasion of Europe this, the only sensible route, was denied to us. We therefore had to struggle across jungle-covered mountains, with no roads through them. And we had to face months of drenching monsoon rains as well.

So we had to rely on air supply on an unprecedented scale

and this was only possible by beating the Japanese Air Force and maintaining air supremacy.

I agreed with my commanders-in-chief that they would process recommendations for decorations and awards through their own service ministries and could quote my fullest support. The army authorities looked after recognition for their forces admirably. The army commander and corps commanders all received knighthoods, and appropriate awards were given to divisional commanders and officers below them. Yet the R.A.F. authorities failed signally to give adequate recognition to their own service, without which the army could never have begun to drive the Japanese out of Burma.

So I am glad to be able to pay my personal tribute to all that the air forces achieved in Burma, the greatest achievements I know of in any theatre of war.

Mountbatten of Burma

A.F.

1

'The take-off'

The Army invited me to join and 'see the world'. The song told us that the Navy 'sees the sea'. I joined the Third Service and saw the world and the sea and the sky and the clouds, my fellow-men and—life.

I caught the fever of flying at a very early age when I frequently dreamt I was flying—by flapping my arms and gliding with them outstretched! Then came the Wright brothers' flight and I transferred my ideas to manufactured wings and engines and started making models at school. Many of my early school-friends had the usual longing to be engine drivers, but I scorned that earth-bound urge and had thoughts only of the air. I went to Hendon and watched the early pioneers there and read all I could about it—but knew that learning to fly was highly improbable for me as my parents were not wealthy and extremely unlikely to pay the necessary fees with no apparent 'investment' therein.

My first close-up of an aeroplane was in 1910 at Shoreham, where my father, brother and I went frequently during our month in a bungalow on the beach, to the aerodrome. There a middle-aged man—H. H. Piffard—had constructed a box-kite type of flying machine with a four-cylinder E.N.V. engine driving a pusher propeller. It was a very elementary machine, front and back elevators, dead flat planes (with no camber) and drooping ailerons with no compensating cable. The pilot controlled it from a position on the bottom main plane, sitting on what looked like a deck-chair without any canvas! There was only one 'perch'. There was one paid mechanic—a Frenchman—and two volunteers, one a fitter, Ouinch, for the engine, and the other a rigger, Sutton, for the airframe. These two had answered an advertisement and were there for the fun of the thing and experience.

Piffard, a nervous individual who smoked non-stop, was not everyone's idea of an intrepid young bird-man, but did manage to do 'straights' of about half a mile in length and some twenty feet off the ground. He was short-sighted and therefore never quite certain when to cut off his engine to land when coming back to the little shed, so that one of us, usually Ouinch, used to stand out in the middle and blow a shrill blast on a whistle, which Piffard could hear above the noise of the engine, close the throttle and land. On one occasion the Humming Bird—as it was called—was just starting the return trip when the whistle could not be found. In panic we all ran out whistling, but could not achieve the required pitch. Fortunately a bell tent took the strain of his late landing.

One day the engine was running really well and his helpers expressed a wish for a revolution counter to know what to aim for in tuning the engine.

My father, a Doctor of Music, said, 'Well, that was "G" '; he then proceeded to town where he bought a 'G' tuning fork, and the engine was subsequently tuned up to this!

The engine would be run up and when humming at full speed everyone would hum and sustain that note while the engine was switched off and the tuning fork twanged and matched. If the notes agreed, then off on another 'straight'; but if it were a semitone or worse out of tune—then out would come the sparking plugs for a clean and a new test until the right note was obtained.

One day Piffard missed the plank bridge over one of the dikes and in he went: struts and spars broken fore and aft and, more seriously, the propeller had one of its two blades splintered into two pieces. The spars could be 'glued, screwed and bound' to as good as new, but the propeller presented more of a problem. The pieces were well glued and held together by three bolts whose heads and nuts protruded, so, to make it a smooth finish, it was bound and glued and covered with an old pair of dungaree trousers. That put the propeller badly out of balance, so three bolts were put into the good blade in carefully measured corresponding positions to the smashed one, and a similar length of dungarees also stuck on! The fine balance necessary was achieved by gluing pieces of dungarees and finally coats of paint. The aeroplane was in the air again well within a week, although we were warned not to stand in line with the propeller when the engine was running on the ground!

One day it was going so well at the end of a 'straight' that Piffard decided to do a circuit . . . He came out of hospital three months later! This was the sad end of the Humming Bird. I learnt a great deal, however, in this short period, and had a lot of fun too. Sutton and Ouinch had supper with us one night, after which we played paper games. One, a fold-over and pass-on game, consisted of a noun, an adjective, and a question. The object then being to write a verse answering the question and bringing in the noun and the adjective. Sutton—I have always remembered—had 'Magneto', 'Snowy white' and 'Are we, as a nation, degenerate?' In two minutes he turned in:

> A snowy-white aeroplane once on a day
> Took to its wings and flew right away.
> The magneto went wrong
> And the man with a frown
> Said, 'If we're not degenerate, I'm going down.'

Officially, I suppose, it does not strictly answer the question, but it was a very fine effort.

Alas, I never did that 'straight' flight with Piffard before the crash as he had planned, as I was the smallest and lightest of his following.

Then came the war in 1914 and I saw my chance to be taught to fly free, if only the war would not finish too soon. It was said that the Germans couldn't afford more than six months—or a year at the most. So, early in 1915, when I was 17 years old, I went to the War Office to volunteer for the Royal Flying Corps where, having, said I could ride a horse, I was accepted after a medical examination.

'Match this piece of wool with a similar one in that pile. Right, what colour is it?'

'Red.'

'Well, I should call it crimson.'

'Well, crimson is red.'

'Oh, I suppose so.'

So, with a few thumps on the chest and listen to heart and lungs, ten minutes saw me through. I then had to mark time for many months before being called up near the end of 1915. I left school—Lancing—and, incidentally, a sanatorium bed with jaundice, and reported to Brooklands where I was put on the books and sent off home for a fortnight's sick leave, which I felt was not a very bright start to my service career!

The pupils there were still civilians until they obtained the Royal Aero Club certificate. Then they would be commissioned which, with their all-important pay, would be antedated to the day of joining. Billets and transport had to be found. There was no mess or club room of any sort; it was hangars or nothing! Fortunately I had a 4 h.p. Bradbury single-geared, single-cylinder motorcycle, with no clutch, so that the starting was a somewhat tricky business. One had to clutch the valve lifter and push, getting up as much speed as possible before letting the lever down when, with a loud bang, the bike would leap forward, probably into a ditch, with the pusher into the one on the other side! A lucky, if painful, leap into the saddle could send one jerking forwards at a rapidly increasing rate until a smooth speed was reached, when the bike did go quite fast and was reasonably reliable.

My first flight was with the 'G' Flight Commander at Brooklands, Captain Stokes, in a Maurice Farman 'Longhorn' pusher biplane with a 70 h.p. Renault engine. My immediate impression was how soon a wonderful view was obtained even at the slow rate of climb of that ancient pusher 'box kite', and that flying was certainly for me what I had anticipated.

A Sergeant Major pilot was detailed as my instructor. He must have been the world's worst flying instructor bar none! I was, as were all pupils, flown round in large left-hand circuits —never right—and I never did more than feel the controls while he flew the machine. In the Maurice Farman 'Longhorn' there were no duplicate controls in a pupil's cockpit; the pupil sat jammed up tight behind the instructor, reaching round his body to get his hands on two handles below those of the pilot (known as a 'pair of spectacles' as they were really segments of a wheel) and which functioned together. The rudders were controlled by pedals, and the pupil did have a pair of these in addition to those of the instructor. In order to get the feel of the

Dual instruction in the 'Longhorn'

moving controls the pupil with his arms stretched round the instructor, had his right ear pressed firmly up against his neck. As both wore enormous safety helmets, the pupil could only see out to the side in an uncomfortable and unnatural left-sided crouch!

We were soon doing take-offs and landings. If the Sergeant Major made a good landing he praised me, and if bad he swore at me lustily, so I just eased my hands off my handles altogether and it was 'mixture as before' until I complained to the Flight

Commander and he, bless him, took me away from this instructor and gave me to a different one when I did have actual control for about ten minutes, including a landing.

He then said, 'Oh well, you get in the front seat.'

I changed over and found myself in an entirely different position with quite a different view, almost like being in a different aeroplane.

I waited for him to get in the back seat but he said, 'Oh no, you are on your own now—good luck!' So after less than $2\frac{1}{2}$ hours in the air of which I don't think I had control for more than fifteen minutes, I was solo and finding myself really enjoying the experience.

Although I subsequently flew well over a hundred different types of aircraft, I never had any more 'Dual'. The following day I was sent up to get my Royal Aero Club Certificate. This consisted of doing two figures of 8 and a landing, repeated again and followed by an 'altitude test' with a landing, from this height without using the engine, within a hundred yards of a mark. My figures of 8 were a reasonably small left-hand circle followed by an enormous one to the right—I had never carried out this before—not even with an instructor—as the torque from the large wooden propeller resisted it and a bank of more than a few degrees was extremely rare. However, by banking about ten degrees to the left and possibly five degrees to the right, we skidded round, and 'got away with it'.

The 'altitude test' was to 500 feet! This was all right, but the landing without the engine running presented a new problem as the usual tree over which we normally throttled back to land was of little help at this height and I found myself overshooting the white sheet landing point. However, by wriggling in left and right turns on the way down I did, in fact, land only about ten yards from the sheet and made my waiting instructor run.

I was congratulated on obtaining my 'ticket' but told off for doing such a dangerous thing as to turn BOTH WAYS with the engine off! Then, with no more trips with an instructor, I flew six hours solo on a 'Longhorn' and six more on a 'Shorthorn'; the latter the same type of aeroplane but without a front elevator. This was a loss to the pupil as the front elevator was a big help to the novice, as by 'keeping it lined up on the horizon' he did not stall (lose flying speed) or climb too steeply.

The poor state of training at that time was emphasised by the next soloist taking off after me who, on reaching the first turning point, apparently put on bank one way and the rudder the other way, with the result that the bank increased until he side-slipped down on to a house where both caught fire. Of all the unimaginative things to do, the pupils were sent out to bring in the remains before even the charred corpse had been removed!

While at Brooklands, the pupils had to assemble a 'Longhorn' from assorted bits and pieces in crates and eventually fly it. The story told was that you built it round a canary, and if it got out, then a wire must be missing! There certainly was a great number of wires, and each had to be in the correct position and properly tensioned, so that the wings were at the right angle of dihedral, incidence and so on. My particular job was to install the control wires, seemingly miles of piano wire and cable, over countless pulleys and so easy to get crossed and so get reversed controls. However, all went well, and it subsequently proved one of the best aeroplanes to fly.

Tim Morice was a contemporary of mine there, who later distinguished himself in both wars, and also McCubbin who was credited later with shooting down the German ace Immelmann.

On one side of Brooklands was the famous—or infamous—sewage farm (inside the track, not outside as depicted in that great film *Those Magnificent Men in their Flying Machines*). One day a pupil, gliding in to land, found he was undershooting. Instead of opening up his engine to carry him over, he tried to extend his glide by 'holding on', with the result that he subsided into it, and turning over was left hanging in his belt with his helmeted head poised just above the terra infirma! The rest of us stood on the edge only about fifteen yards away shouting encouragement and assorted advice. After a time he loosened his belt and fell in head first up to his shoulders, to the cheers of the audience. He waded to the side and left for a bath and a change while the job of rescuing the 'Shorthorn' started, winching it in on a line of planks.

On another day I saw Harry Hawker, the Sopwith test pilot, fly under the footbridge over the track in a Sopwith Tabloid, forerunner of the famous Sopwith Pup. A small aeroplane, fortunately, as there was remarkably little space under the bridge.

Having completed my twelve hours' solo, I was granted my commission (and pay) as from my date of joining, and left for Beaulieu, in the New Forest, to learn to fly tractor biplanes—those with the engine and airscrew in front, pulling the machines instead of pushing as with the Farmans at Brooklands. Here I was to fly the B.E.2C and Avro biplanes, the former with 70 h.p. Renault stationary and the latter with 50 h.p. Gnôme rotary engines. My instructor was Captain Hereward de Havilland who took me up once in the front seat of a non-dual control B.E.—then sent me off solo in the quite different view back seat!

We had a marquee beside the aerodrome for a mess, and one full moon night the weather was so perfect that de Havilland said, 'I'm going to fly, it's so beautiful.'

Without having time to think I asked, 'May I too?'

Somewhat surprised, he answered, 'All right, take a 2C and good luck to you.'

With only an hour or two experience off I went, with no flare-path and only the somewhat confusing light of the full moon. It was wonderful; absolutely calm and the lights of Southampton and smaller villages made it all very dramatic—it was before black-out times. Coming in to land, I could see while gliding in all the other pupils standing outside the mess-tent hopefully waiting for the pile-up! I gave them a shout of glee as I swished past.

Beaulieu aerodrome had been made on a heath from which heather had been burnt off and was consequently jet black except for patches of bright yellow where large holes had been filled in with sand and gravel. Seeing only blackness beneath gave the impression that I was still high off the surface, and so pushed the stick forward only to see a yellow patch suddenly appear close, so hastily I pulled the stick back to prevent flying into the ground. Then, blackness again, so by sheer luck, by alternately pushing the stick forward and pulling it back, I happened to bring off a perfect 'three pointer'—that is with the main undercarriage wheels and the tail skid all touching down together. So no bouncing, to my delight—and to the surprise and disappointment of the crowd who could hear the steady continuous rumble of a good landing.

We had to do our cross-country flight to Shoreham which, being along the coast all the way, was scarcely a severe test of navigation. One gallant, however, did manage to get himself lost over the sea somehow. Instead of doing the obvious thing, and steering due north to regain the coast, he flew round a trawler shouting 'Where's England?' Not surprisingly they could not, of course, hear—or reply; so he shut off his engine and ditched a perfectly serviceable aeroplane alongside. He was sent in turn, to England, the infantry and France, and in fairly rapid succession.

After about another twelve hours or so on B.E.2Cs and Avros, we had to go to the Central Flying School at Upavon on Salisbury Plain to get our 'wings'. This consisted of a written exam in the morning on engines and rigging, and an oral in the afternoon (a walk round the workshop and 'What is this?' 'Oh, that is a Renault connecting-rod' was about the limit of my exam), and a 'Buzzing Exam' when we had to pass at eight words a minute on the Morse Code, followed by flying a 'Service type' for an hour. The 'Service type' was a B.E.2C we had already flown, but with a 90 h.p. R.A.F. engine (R.A.F. for Royal Aircraft Factory) instead of the 70 h.p. Renault, so this did not present much of a difficulty. Then with wings proudly on the tunic (and what a great improvement that made to the 'maternity jacket' of the R.F.C.) I went on to fly scouts at Gosport, having been recommended for that élite arm of those days as I had not broken anything.

The 'scouts' at Gosport were as unscoutlike as they could possibly be; less so, than the Avro I had been flying at Beaulieu. The first I flew was an old Blériot monoplane, slow and sluggish on the controls, which 'went up by the grace of God and came down by the action of gravity'. I was 'shown the taps' by an instructor standing on the wing beside the cockpit, while another soloist was having similar instruction a few yards away. Our information was 'Don't climb under 50 m.p.h., and don't glide under 60.' My neighbour was a minute or two before me and I had great difficulty taking off as I had to dodge those running out to his body in the middle of the aerodrome . . . he had climbed under 50!

The Blériot Parasol and Morane Parasol were the only other types there. These had their monoplane wings above the fuselage, hence their name; they did give therefore a very good downwards view—but neither were scouts. The Blériots had 50 h.p. Gnôme rotary engines and the Morane an 80 h.p. Le Rhône rotary which was a great improvement on the Gnôme as it could be throttled down, by juggling with the air and petrol levers to get the correct mixture, whereas the Gnôme was either 'on' or 'off'.

So—not having flown a genuine single-seater, never done a turn of over 45 degrees of bank, never fired a machine-gun in the air, nor had any lecture or instruction in air fighting, off I went to France as a scout pilot!

Also at Gosport, but in No. 27 Reserve Squadron, was a famous character of those days, a Captain Gordon Bell, who stuttered, and about whom are many stories. He had had a successful encounter with the Assistant Provost Marshal of Portsmouth and Southsea, and a little later found himself sitting in the adjacent seat to him in a barber's shop.

The A.P.M.'s barber finished shortly before Gordon Bell's and proffered some hair oil to him. The sour-faced A.P.M. asked to smell it, so a few drops were waved in front of his nose on the barber's hand, to get his reply: 'Good Lord, no! My wife would think I'd been in a brothel.'

When Gordon Bell's barber then finished, the same procedure exactly was followed, with Gordon Bell's reply: 'Y-y-yes, I'll h-h-have s-s-some of that, m-m-my wife d-d-d-doesn't know what a brothel smells like!'

2

Learning to fight

In May 1916 I went to France by boat and train, and having reported to No. 1 Aircraft Depot at St. Omer, was sent on almost immediately to No. 60 Squadron, R.F.C., at Le Vert Galand on the Amiens–St. Pol road. I went as a reserve pilot in the Squadron which had only been in France about a month. In the Crossley tender on the way from the station, I was told by the driver that already I was no longer in reserve, as the Squadron had suffered its first casualty—no less than its Commanding Officer, Major 'Ferdy' Waldron, who had, he told me, been shot down and killed by our own anti-aircraft fire.

The Squadron consisted of two flights of Morane Saulnier single-seater monoplanes and one of two-seater biplanes from the same French firm. The little monoplane was very similar to the Fokker monoplanes, so our own aircraft and anti-aircraft batteries often fired at it. So did the Germans, and we were more or less under fire from the time we took off to the time we landed, on both sides of the lines. To identify ourselves we painted the 'spinners' on the propellers red, and later, all of the cowling, undercarriage and wheels in the same way; this did stop a great deal of the 'friendly' fire!

The Morane Bullet, as it was known, was a strange and initially a difficult aeroplane to fly as it had warp controlled wings; this meant that the whole wing had to be twisted by cables above and below and was consequently very heavy on the controls laterally. Then the elevators had no fixed tail plane and being 'balanced' about one-third of their length from the front, were therefore very sensitive indeed; also the rudder was too small, requiring more footwork than most. Very considerable effort had to be put into banking the aeroplane, and very little indeed for nose up or down. The armament consisted of one Lewis gun, just in front of the pilot, firing through the propeller arc; but there was no gearing to prevent the bullets hitting the propeller, so two metal deflector plates were bolted on the blades. Those were 'V' shaped, with their apex facing toward the gun. It was estimated that about one in every seventeen rounds fired hit this deflector plate and shot off to one side, not encouraging formation flying! The ammunition was in drums of 47 rounds—later these were enlarged to take 97, and as the gun was immediately in front of the pilot he was able to load and sight and also to work at the many stoppages which frequently occurred.

Captain Robert Smith-Barry—soon to be promoted to Major—had taken over command of No. 60, the Flight Commanders were Captains 'Jimmy' Tower and Summers, and Lieutenant Simpson. I was posted to fill the vacancy in 'A' Flight, and was sent up on my first evening by Smith-Barry to do two 'stalls' and two landings. The entire squadron turned out of their tents alongside the field—only about 400 by 200 yards—anticipating a crash. I got off in a somewhat undulating manner due to the sensitive elevator and did two very gentle 'stalls', which did, at least, show me the slowest speed at which it was safe to glide. I then managed my two landings (to the general disappointment) so, after ten rather shaky minutes, I climbed out to be told by the C.O.: 'Right, Vincent, you'll be on the dawn patrol tomorrow.' He used the French pronunciation of my name, after the somewhat notorious Café Vincent in St. Omer, and as such I was thereafter known.

So, with remarkably little knowledge of my mount—other than the 80 h.p. Le Rhône engine which I had used in England—never having fired a gun in the air and with complete ignorance of air fighting, off I went at first light next morning.

The only 'fighting' advice I had from Smith-B (as he was always known) was sound and I always tried to keep to it—'Don't fire your gun until you are certain of hitting; don't think the enemy will be frightened by the sound of firing, he will know if you are likely to hit him from the position of your aeroplane. He will, on the other hand, get scared if you are silently and relentlessly holding your fire until you are certain of results, and don't fire until you are at really close range.'

It happened that on that first occasion we—six of us—were escorting a long-range reconnaissance-cum-bombing raid and were were strung out above R.E. and B.E. aircraft from two squadrons in our wing. I was on the extreme right and never even saw the solitary Fokker which appeared for a short threat on the other flank. I was too busy reading my map and seeing the scars made across the country by the trenches and finding such famous places as Albert, Cambrai, Douai and St. Quentin over which we flew. What 'Archie'—anti-aircraft fire—there was, was directed at the two-seaters below so I only saw the black splodges and heard fairly distant pops. I felt that the war wasn't so bad and that I had had a very fortunate initiation.

Our normal day was of three Offensive Patrols, about five to ten miles over the other side of the lines, in order to protect our B.E. artillery observation aircraft from attacks by enemy fighters. We usually did these in pairs, up and down a fifteen to twenty miles' stretch of front. This was varied with escort duties for bombing raids by F.E.s or B.E.s which, in order to carry bombs, had frequently to go without their air-gunners and were even more vulnerable than usual. I think I almost enjoyed these duties by feeling a great sense of responsibility towards the solitary pilots in their sitting targets.

My first fight, coming quite soon, had its amusing and also lucky aspect. There were six of us, which was rare in mid-1916 when we normally operated in pairs on a Deep Offensive Patrol flying Morane Bullets. When about a dozen miles over the lines on the Somme front, we saw seven aeroplanes coming towards us, and all of us thought they were 'Elephant' Martinsydes of No. 27 Squadron. In turn, I imagine that they thought we were Fokker monoplanes, as we converged in a friendly supporting manner. It was not until we were almost passing that I saw that they had black crosses and my heart gave a jump of pre-fight fear. One of the seven, well behind the others, shut off his engine, turned and dived away. My immediate thought was 'Oh, you cur!' as he had the choice of being two to one if we all paired off and he had the best chance of all of us. This made me forget my fear and also made me furious, so I turned in towards the enemy and dashed through in lonely ignorance. Having got beyond them without getting anything in my gun-sight, I eventually did pair off with one and we started a large gentle left-hand turn and were going round on the circumference of a fairly wide circle.

Our leader, Captain Simpson, as soon as he had realised that the other formation was enemy, endeavoured to signal us. Trying to grip his control column with his knees, find his Very pistol and fire a red cartridge, he fell into a spin. Spinning, then, was almost certain death. He clutched the stick to his stomach to try to pull the nose up, which made the spin all the faster. He shut his engine off, and after a time let go of the controls in desperation, whereupon his little monoplane got itself out of the spin and dived straight. Simpson then levelled out some thousands of feet below the rest of us but, being in a monoplane, he had a perfect view of what was happening above while struggling to climb back. This was probably a ten-minute job at over 10,000 feet.

I was still gently circling with my gun always facing about 90 degrees away from my waltzing partner. He was in an L.V.G. two-seater and I could hear his rear-gunner firing away at me pop-pop-pop—but when this turned to ack-ack-ack I realised I was hearing bullets, not the gun, and that they were very close indeed to my head. One of the warp control wires in front of me was suddenly cut then my windscreen (just in front of my face) shattered and I came to the conclusion that I was losing this particular bit of war and must do something desperate, in fact attempt a 'split-arse turn', although I had never banked over 45 degrees before! I pushed the stick well over and then pulled, whereupon the little Morane spun round with the greatest of ease and I was turning well inside my opponent and cutting him off.

He was probably an even worse and less experienced pilot

than I, for he did the worst thing possible by coming out of his gentle left-hand turn and going into one to the right, thus lining up straight in front of me. My gun-sight was suddenly full for the first time. I opened fire and saw the pilot throw his hand up over his head—he was about fifty yards away—and then my gun jammed. I felt helpless and turned westward towards the lines while I tried feverishly to correct the stoppage. I eventually found it was a bulged drum, replaced it, and turned back to join in the war once more, only to find a completely empty sky. No sign of friend or foe.

Hanging about for a bit I was joined, to my relief, by Simpson, who had climbed back to our height, then Reggie Smart—and at the end of our patrol time we flew back to Vert Galand, north of Amiens. Later the other three, D. V. Armstrong, Meintzes and Gilchrist, returned, one with a shot-away tappet rod having landed at one of our aerodromes to have it repaired, followed by the others. To my surprise Simpson ran up to me and congratulated me on shooting down the L.V.G. He had seen the scrap from below and then seen the enemy go down into the ground. I had only fired seventeen rounds of ammunition, as we found by checking my bulged drum, so I must have hit the pilot with my first short burst.

A little later the farmer, his wife and daughter, in whose barn-loft we were sleeping, carried in a bunch of flowers with a paper attached—*'Felicitations au Lieutenant Vincent'*. This paper now figures in No. 60 Squadron's History Book in recognition of the first of the many enemy aircraft shot down by the Squadron.

I was, of course, very lucky. The enemy gunner might so easily have got my head instead of the windscreen—so near on one side, or the petrol tank or engine, so close the other way. In the latter case I could not have reached the lines as we were too far over, and I would have been taken prisoner or killed without having fired a shot myself. Instead I learnt that the aeroplane could do much more, if asked, and I was able to ask it on many subsequent occasions until I became 'quite a pilot'.

After this experience I improved considerably as a pilot and my confidence grew until I felt—when later having a similar personal scrap—'I'm a better pilot than he is and I know he's afraid of me'; I could feel it. This was greatly due to Smith-B's original advice—silently and ominously hanging on to an inevitable conclusion—or at least, so I hoped!

3

Flights and fights

For some reason No. 60 Squadron was selected to deliver a French spy behind the lines, and Claud Ridley was detailed to fly him in a Morane Biplane. Several reconnaissance trips were made to choose the most suitable field for landing: one in the spy's own familiar country, large enough to permit a take-off again and near a wood in which the passenger could quickly hide. When the day came several of us were instructed to fly low in an area of about ten miles radius, so that the one important aeroplane would not be so conspicuous in flying low to make its landing. Unfortunately, just as Ridley was about to go down, his engine cut out and he had to land immediately in the chosen field. Not being able to take off again he set fire to his aeroplane, and ran with the Frenchman into the wood, where they evaded capture for the next few days by hiding up trees. The spy then went on his way but brought back civilian clothes for Ridley, before he finally left to carry out his mission. Ridley then spent some two months in enemy territory before eventually crossing over the border into Holland after many adventures. He brought with him much useful information for which he was awarded a D.S.O.

No. 60 Squadron suffered very heavy casualties during the Somme offensive and we were taken out of the line to re-equip and re-form at an aerodrome near Montreuil where Army G.H.Q. was located. King George V came to visit the Headquarters and we were detailed to maintain an all-day patrol overhead to prevent any hostile attack. All other squadrons had been notified that this was a prohibited area, so anything seen over or approaching the town would be considered to be hostile.

While doing my stint in a Morane Biplane, Bryant, my observer, suddenly banged me on the back and pointed feverishly downwards. There, sure enough, I saw a biplane flying very low, just approaching the town. I dived steeply towards it to find it was an 'Elephant' Martinsyde. The pilot, I heard later, having forced landed two days previously a few miles from the town, had not heard of the prohibition. I flew alongside and waved him away; a gesture the pilot did not at first understand, but eventually he got the message and turned off. The episode was seen at G.H.Q. and the Squadron got a pat on the back for being alert.

We flew to our next war station in what was, I believe, the first squadron formation of single-seater fighters, as we had taken on our first Nieuport Scouts in the place of the Morane two-seater biplanes. The Nieuports were what the French called sesquiplanes, as they were really one and a half planes—the lower wing being very narrow and shorter than the top main plane. They were very pleasant to fly, very manœuvrable, with a good view and a better performance, speed and climb, than the Morane Bullets.

On arrival at our new station—Fillescamps—which we were to share with No. 11 Squadron (F.E.2Bs) no less than four members turned over on their backs or tipped up on their noses while landing. I was in a Morane Bullet and had landed satisfactorily so sat up on the fuselage behind the cockpit with goggles pushed up to the top of my head looking as dramatic and important as possible and said to the assembled members of the local squadron that, of course, these were very difficult aircraft to fly and land and only the very finest—like me, for instance—could manage to cope! Excusable? I wonder! One of those 'nose tippers' was Albert Ball in his Nieuport who had recently joined the Squadron and already had a good 'offensive' reputation.

The Nieuport's armament—and we were soon completely re-equipped with these good little aeroplanes—was still one

Lewis gun, but in this case mounted on the centre section of the top plane firing over the top of the propeller. A quadrant mounting allowed the gun to be slid down to fire anywhere between straight ahead and vertically upwards. Ball made great use of the ability to fire upwards, and would fly close below an enemy two-seater where he could not be fired at and would shoot down his opponent from beneath.

On one occasion he had run out of ammunition while attacking a German formation well over the enemy lines. When I asked him how he had managed to escape after that, he said he had spotted one two-seater facing towards the lines and slid underneath it so close that the pilot dared not bank for fear of collision, and the remaining ones could not fire at him for fear of hitting their comrade! When they neared the lines he dived away, having first fired a Very light at it—but without any result apart from showing bravado.

Soon we were moved to Savy just behind Arras to cover that offensive, as we had done previously on the Somme. Ball lived in a little hut on the aerodrome close to his Nieuport with only his violin for company, and was known as the 'lonely Ball' (or almost this!). When he went on leave for seven days and my machine was in dock for repairs or engine change, I flew his Nieuport. His aircraft was distinct from the others by a red spinner on the propeller. This aircraft was evidently well known to the enemy as I couldn't get near one during this week! They fled on seeing the red spinner and I, accordingly, felt very brave but did little to help.

While at Savy I could have achieved everlasting fame as the one who shot down Richthofen—the Red Baron—but . . . We were escorting half a dozen F.E.2Bs of No. 11 Squadron back from a photographic reconnaissance flight to Douai, when—as usually happened at this time—we were attacked by Richthofen's unit, in two flights. Our Nieuports were 1,000 feet above the F.E.s when the first attack came in from astern where the F.E.s were blind; we dived down on to the attackers who turned away.

While we were climbing back to our original protective position, the second flight took the opportunity to make a similar attack. The F.E.s took their normal action and turned to face the enemy with a clear field of fire and support from each other to force the Albatrosses to break off their attack. The F.E.s would then quickly turn back westwards and the whole procedure would have to be repeated again and again.

On this occasion I noticed one Albatross leave the others and go out to one flank and, turning to the west, gradually circle round with the obvious intention of attacking the F.E.s in the rear while they were facing east and the remainder of the enemy. Keeping my eye on this opportunist I dived on him when he started in to attack, but misjudging our approaching speeds found myself getting steeper and steeper in my dive, with my bullets obviously going behind him. Then I saw it was the Red Baron himself in his all-red fighter, and I had at least stopped his wary attack, and we started a private and personal battle, circling round, up and down, trying to get behind one another.

I like to think I may have got a few holes in his aeroplane: he certainly got none in mine, though I heard his guns firing. I don't know how long this would have continued if Roderick Hill (later to become famous and to reach high rank) hadn't joined in. With the odds of two to one, Richthofen dived away and we returned to the circling, diving, and climbing 'mixture as before'. All our aircraft returned, but so too did all the enemy. This often happened when about two dozen or so were involved and our fighters had an escorting job to do and could not leave it to go chasing after a lame duck or a singleton.

One evening when it was raining hard and the clouds were down to a few hundred feet, precluding the possibility of any flying, a few of us thought of going into Amiens for dinner at the Hôtel du Rhin. I was deputed to get permission from the C.O. for a Crossley tender for the evening, as I could understand better than the others that Smith-B's bark was so much worse than his bite.

My request was greeted by, 'How dare you come and ask me this? Don't you realise there is a war on? We may be called out any moment to fly, fight . . .'

When he had finished I replied, 'All right, sir, if you say so.

We only thought there would be no chance of being called upon,' by which time I had backed to the door.

He continued, 'How many did you say there were of you?'

'Four, sir.'

'Well, how dare you come and ask for a tender—take my tourer.'

We enjoyed our evening.

On another occasion three of us, on offensive patrol, ran into a large number of the enemy. We got into a furious scrap for nearly half an hour after which we were lucky to find each other when the sky suddenly cleared of enemy—as it did in a miraculous manner—probably due to their fuel running low. We flew round for a short time feeling pretty 'done' and then D. V. Armstrong led us to the lines and home, to my great relief and I imagine that of Meintjies, the South African.

We landed and climbed out while our ground crews looked for the expected holes in the aircraft. The C.O. met us, called us aside, and while still in our leather coats and fur-lined boots, he gave us an imperial ticking-off. He pointed out that we were fifteen minutes early, that German fighters were now probably shooting down our Artillery Observation craft, that they were killing our soldiers in the trenches, that we were letting the Squadron down, and were, in fact, losing the war. I felt it a bit unfair, personally, having followed my leader and I took it hard, being only eighteen, so crept off to the 'Buck Tent' which was a marquee bar at the side and dejectedly sat in a deck-chair. Before long Smith-B came in, walked up to me and said, 'Hello, Vincent!' (giving the French pronunciation). 'Have a brandy.' He knew. And his action did me a power of good.

The cold is one of my chief recollections of those patrols, although we wore one or two woollies, a leather coat, silk and wool gloves inside leather gauntlets, silk and wool socks inside fur-lined thigh-length boots, a woollen Balaclava helmet inside a leather one, and goggles so that only the nose showed. Sitting in an open cockpit with only a thin fabric surround and no heat from the small air-cooled rotary engine, we steadily froze into a state of numbness. This lasted until coming down from some fifteen thousand feet to the comparative 'warmth' of about three thousand feet, where the pain was acute in the fingers and toes when the blood thawed, and it was almost agony to keep hands and feet on the controls.

I found that 'the heat of battle' was not an idle phrase. However frozen when starting a scrap, I found when it was finished, after twenty-five or thirty minutes, I would be perfectly warm all over without having noticed the change and consequent pain. I was not—and am not—'brave'. I was thoroughly scared beforehand and on one occasion was physically sick on the way to the aeroplane; but when I started in a fight, the excitement and sense of competition made me almost enjoy it. I rejoiced at seeing an enemy aeroplane shot down—it was a 'thing'. But on one occasion when I shot a two-seater off the tail of an F.E., in flames, I saw the observer jump out—no parachutes at that time—and I suddenly realised that it was a personal affair and the sight sickened me.

While at Savy I found there were several instrumentalists in the Squadron and decided to form a band. I bought an excellent upright piano in St. Omer for a very good pianist, Sergeant Nicod, and from that basis gradually worked up to about fifteen performers on an assortment of instruments obtained through my father's efforts in advertising in musical papers, and gifts. We played on many occasions and at other squadrons; also at the Third Army Boxing Tournament. At Major Smith-Barry's farewell dinner on being posted home, a special hut was erected and senior officers from Army, Wing, Anti-aircraft and local squadrons attended. It was a great affair and I dashed from eating to conducting, but I like to think that the band made the evening. Unfortunately, it came to be considered unlucky for an officer to be in the band, as one after another they got killed. Roderick Hill—on the fiddle—stayed longest, although he gave it up for that reason.

The Squadron shared Savy aerodrome with No. 13 Squadron (night-flying B.E.s). We were in the 13th Wing under Colonel 'Pip' Playfair, and twice while I was with the Squadron there was Friday the 13th. On one of these days, before a dawn patrol, I lit my cigarette third from a match, so I was considered lost for certain (I had also earlier on smashed my shaving-mirror). However, when I returned—still living and not worried—I was asked by an agonised superstitious member to do his mid-day patrol, in exchange for 'three next week'.

This safe return so impressed a second member of the Squadron that he—going through agonies of superstition—asked exactly the same thing for the dusk patrol! Again I went out and back, and so had a promise of six in return; I only asked, however, for one patrol from each. It availed nothing for the second man, I fear, as he was killed shortly afterwards on a very ordinary day and date.

We had a Scottish orderly who used to travel round on his P & M motorcycle at about 01.00 hrs, leave it spluttering and banging on its stand outside while he came up into the barn where we were billeted, and shaking my shoulder would say, 'I'm sorry to inforrrm you, sirrrr, but you are on earrly patrrol; I'll call you at four.' Seemingly only a few minutes had elapsed when he came back to say it was 'fourr'. Then, with the other one or two similarly aroused, we would put on our 'maternity jackets' over pyjamas, with the usual woollies, and extras and get on our way. Returning, we hoped, about 07.00 hrs, we would get back into bed for another hour or two and start the day fresh—our dawn patrol being considered almost as yesterday. My Scottish warning and awakening is still a very vivid memory.

The Squadron did a balloon strafe one day using Le Prier rockets of which four were fixed on each side to the interplane struts, fired electrically by a button on the joystick. George Philippi, landing after making his attack, had his engine stop before taxying in. His fitter who ran out to swing the propeller to restart the engine yelled 'Ambulance!' Running out, we found him unconscious in his seat.

We lifted him out, which was not an easy job as he was a big man and the Nieuport's cockpit was very small. Examining him, we could find nothing wrong at first, but then noticed his helmet was damaged, and when removed revealed a big bruise oozing blood high on his forehead. From the machine it appeared that a shell had passed through the mainplane and brushed against his head as it shot by. A fraction inwards and it would have cracked his skull and might have burst as well. As it was, he was concussed and flew back—having shot down his balloon satisfactorily—to the right aerodrome and landed perfectly normally before losing consciousness.

Remembering nothing of what had happened, Philippi came in to the evening meal with us and went to bed early. He slept in a small room in the local Mayor's house in Savy. Smith-Barry called on him the following morning on his way to breakfast and found him sitting up in bed with a loaded revolver in his hand, looking somewhat wild.

The major said, 'Well, George, what sort of night did you have?'

To which George replied, 'Oh, all right, except for This and That' (not the accurate nicknames of two unpopular 'yellow' officers in the Squadron), 'they would keep on coming in, and when I tried to shoot them they'd jump out of the window and escape.'

The C.O., keeping calm and quiet, said, 'Well, that's lucky, they're downstairs having breakfast. If you give me the revolver I'll go down and shoot them for you and you'll be able to get some sleep.'

Philippi immediately handed over his gun and Smith-Barry left, with relief, and sent the doctor up, who, thereupon, got an ewer full of water right in the face on entry! Poor George had to be sent home, strapped to a stretcher, but in two or three months was quite fit again, the blood clot having dispersed.

A little later 'This' was still having 'oil pressure trouble' or a 'missing engine' just as we reached the lines, and had to return to the aerodrome so, when the Squadron was sent an aerial camera to experiment with, it was put in his machine. H.Q. considered that the poor F.E.s on photo-recce, committed to a straight run at a constant speed and height, were unable to dodge 'Archie' and were having high casualties. It was considered that a Nieuport might be able to do the job while an escort turned and twisted and so not get the same attention from the ground fire and obtain the same result with greater economy.

Three of us were detailed to escort 'This' while he photographed a length of the Hindenburg Line, or something similar. He had to lead but, as to be expected, flew a mile or two short of his target and then tipped his Nieuport up a degree or two hoping to cover the area in this fashion. When developed the film was found to be too distorted; the four of us were summoned before Smith-B and told to go straight out again, instructing the three escorts to fly one on each side and one behind the leader, and should he stray either side of the straight and narrow line, we were to fire our guns—with very visible tracer bullets—past his wing-tips, or above or below, from behind, if he left the exact height. Back we went again and each of us fired at least one burst just to show our displeasure at an unnecessary trip over the lines. The photographs were all right this time, and we were lucky that we did not meet any enemy aircraft.

Soon after 'This' on a similar trip with a different escort had 'engine failure' when well over the lines and went down and landed where he was taken prisoner. We all felt that he thought he would be safer that way and it was preferable to being shot at by friend and foe alike!

Unfortunately the camera was discovered in his aircraft and so Nieuports received far more attention from anti-aircraft fire than before. On one occasion, when well over the other side of the trenches, my own engine had two cylinders cut out making it impossible to keep station with the others. Hopefully I turned back for the lines and home. 'Archie' spotting a lame duck committed to fairly straight flying gave me special and personal attention for about ten miles. By good fortune I was not seen by enemy fighters and when I did cross the lines, at about two thousand feet, I had the satisfaction of observing the long row of black bursts behind me indicating a lot of enemy money spent on me personally without the satisfaction of having made a single hole in my aeroplane.

That was a significant psychological difference between being shelled in the air and the ground. In the air the shells were aimed for you personally, whereas on the ground, they were fired at anybody who might be in their target area. It sometimes did feel very 'personal'. On another occasion I was flying on the right of three aircraft in the usual 'V' formation when a shell burst right in front of my nose—I flew into the evil-smelling blackness and was knocked down about fifty feet or more, appearing out the other side to the intense surprise of the other two, who both thought I had been blown to smithereens. The extraordinary thing was that on examining my machine after we got back later, there was not a single hole in it. It must have been all blast without shrapnel.

I preferred escort duties to any other as I felt a sense of responsibility which was, thereby, a boost to one's ego. On many occasions we had telephone calls from those escorted, thanking us for doing the job. 'Come and have a drink—you've just saved our lives' is a very pleasant message to receive. Some years after the war I was effusively thanked by an ex-B.E. pilot who had been attacked by some Albatros fighters and had pretty well given up all hope of survival when suddenly a flight of Nieuports arrived from high above and chased the enemy away. He had found out afterwards that I was leading the flight, this was after I had taken over 'A' Flight.

Well-known fighters in the squadron included 'Grid' Caldwell, a New Zealander who did well then and better still later on in No. 74 Squadron, E. O. Grenfell who, after his flight had forced down an enemy two-seater on our side of the lines, piled up his Nieuport in landing alongside, breaking his leg, Portal (Chief of the Air Staff in World War II), Reggie Smart, James Latta, Harold Balfour (later Lord Balfour of Inchrye and Under-Secretary of State for Air), Sid Parker, Duncan Bell-Irving, Gilchrist, Weedon, Pidcock, Giles, Fry, Stokes and the new C.O., E. P. Graves, a gallant successor to Smith-Barry but who was unfortunately shot down and killed three months after taking over command. The Squadron had two famous Sergeant Majors, Aspinall, disciplinary, and Smirk, technical. They did much towards the Squadron's history. This history was unfortunately very considerably curtailed when the Squadron H.Q. hut was burnt out completely at Savy, and all the early records destroyed, including the list of enemy aircraft destroyed or damaged—confirmed or otherwise.

I had an unpleasant experience in my machine one day when

the lower port wing twisted two or three degrees in a dive. This could only happen in a Nieuport which had only a single spar in its lower wing, gripped in the fuselage by a somewhat elementary device of a solid wooden circle held by clamps tightened by two nuts only. There was just enough control left, with the stick right over to the side of the cockpit and, by keeping the speed over about 85 m.p.h., for me to get back to Filescamp to make a fast landing with my tail high and pulling up just before overrunning the field. The rigger fixed the spar-slip by a friction pad—two strips of sandpaper round the wood, one facing inwards and the other towards the clamp!

One day when leading the Flight on a dawn patrol, I saw a B.E.12 flying parallel, between us and the rising sun. It looked such easy prey, slow, not very manœuvrable, with no protection behind. Then I saw as it turned that it bore black crosses. Obviously, a captured B.E. being used to deceive us both in the air and on the ground. I swung in to attack thinking that I had the chance I had just been visualising, but he was equally quick in turning away and diving down, so that I was never able to catch up much on the quarter of a mile or more that we had been apart. So back to the patrol line—cursing!

I had an excellent batman, O'Donnell, who saw to my every need; always there was hot water for my canvas bath, bits of furniture appearing from somewhere, including a good oil lamp, although this was a little more than embarrassing when the C.O. came into my room and said, 'Oh, there's my oil lamp!'

I asked O'Donnell what he had been in civilian life before the war and he replied, 'Well, as a matter of fact, sir, I was a burglar!'

Unfortunately as he was of A1 medical category, he was weeded out from his cushy job and transferred to the infantry, and I never heard another word of him. I hope he came through the war; my things were always safe with him—never a cigarette missing. Honour among thieves, perhaps!

4

Instructing instructors

My tour in France finished early in March 1917 just before the 'Bloody April', when the R.F.C.'s casualties rose alarmingly through the Germans introducing new and better fighters. As it was, the personnel in my own squadron had already been replaced nearly three times over in the ten months it had been in France.

Smith-Barry, my previous C.O. in No. 60 Squadron, had left almost in disgrace, because he had complained so much and so frequently about the abysmal state of training of the pilots sent out to fight. Eventually the War Office took note and said, in effect, 'If you think you can do any better, come home and do so.' He was given the training squadrons at Gosport which were formed experimentally into the School of Special Flying—S.S.F. (Some Sticky Finish, as it was rudely called). Firstly Smith-Barry cut out the Farman stage of learning and started pupils on the Avro. The pupil was placed in the seat from which he would fly his first solo, with the instructor in the front. Voice tubes, subsequently known as Gosport tubes, were made for intercommunication, and every movement of the controls and the aeroplane was explained in detail by the instructor. The results were almost immediate, and the first pupils flew their solos with ability and confidence.

Twenty pupils on the list for training taken purposely at random were sent to Gosport for training and, when ready for their solo flights, 'The Great' from the War Office came to watch. Every one flew in front of this audience in an extremely convincing manner, some even looped and everyone landed successfully. They were then given one trip in the latest type of service aircraft and the same performance was repeated, with only one blemish, when one young pilot not appreciating the higher landing speed, overran into the moat of Fort Rowner, without very serious damage, however.

The War Office, duly impressed, arranged for all instructors in every training unit to go on a course at Gosport to learn the new methods. So the first Instructors' School was started and the method spread, gradually, all over the country, and finally all over the world. Smith-Barry did me the honour of applying for me to join him when I came home, and I became one of the first three Flight Commanders together with Sid Parker and Alan Duncan Bell-Irving, also both ex-60 Squadron. Others from the old squadron also joined, George Philippi as Adjutant and Dundas Heanan as Stores Officer.

Flying instructors from all over the world where we had training units—United Kingdom, Canada, South Africa and Australasia—came through a three-week concentrated course. Some arrived complaining that after shooting down ten or so enemy aircraft the idea of being taught to fly was ridiculous, but all left thoroughly humbled and grateful, wondering how they—and their pupils—had managed to survive with so little knowledge.

Another unit at Gosport was teaching pupils to fly the F.E.2B, a pusher biplane with a 120 h.p. Beardmore engine, with a gunner out in front of the pilot who sat with the engine behind him. I had not flown them, so I borrowed one from Major Wells, one of the Flight Commanders. I went off and flew about for a while with an airman as passenger in the front seat. While at about 2,000 feet I thought how unusual it was to feel the heat from the radiator on the back of my neck and then the sun appeared to be reflected on my instruments. But suddenly I realised that the sun was in front of me and could not possibly shine there. Turning, I saw a mass of flame enveloping the engine. Luckily, I was not far from the aerodrome and turned the petrol off and put the machine into a steep dive, thanking my lucky stars that it was a pusher and so fanning the flames away from me. I arrived at one end of the aerodrome and went the full length of it owing to my excessive speed, but by this time I had dived the fire out.

We sat for a moment—my white-faced passenger and I—and then wondered whether we could start up again or not. Deciding that we could now easily jump out if it caught fire again, we started up the engine satisfactorily and taxied in. When I told Major Wells of the incident he laughed and said I wasn't used to the heat of the engine behind. When I expostulated that it wasn't just heat but flame and considerable flame, again he laughed openly and said that we chaps with rotary engines weren't used to the flames from open exhaust pipes. I insisted that this engine was on fire. He refused, however, to be impressed. Then the very next morning, I saw the same F.E.2B coming hurriedly in to land blazing like a furnace, just in time for Major Wells and a pupil to jump clear before the tank exploded and the aeroplane disintegrated.

I was able to go up to Wells and say, 'Oh, that's only the exhaust flame, there's nothing to worry about!'

White-faced and shaking, he replied, 'By God! I deserve to have been burnt up not to have believed you yesterday.'

It was a worth-while job, but, alas! An Avro, usually so strong and reliable, broke up in the air while flying straight and level at a low altitude at 07.30 hrs one Sunday morning at the end of April. I came to in hospital at 15.30 hrs the following Thursday afternoon. After a further seven months in hospital I felt I ought to go back to France again as I hadn't been doing anything to win the war for so long. I was, accordingly, posted to No. 110 Squadron at Dover from where I thought we would soon be leaving for France, that being the obvious stepping-off place.

Before joining I visited Gosport, and Smith-B invited me to take up any aeroplane I liked to see how it felt. I took an Avro and found it was just like it always had been, and very enjoyable it was to be in the air again. Not having any recollection of my crash whatever, my nerve was not affected in any way. I landed in the field into which I had fallen and found the hole and bits of wood still about, and could not imagine how it had happened, and how I had come to be a bloody mess there in a crumpled Avro. I flew out and put it out of my mind.

In the Court of Inquiry into the crash—while I was in hospital—evidence was given that 'something' was seen to fall from the aeroplane and that the bottom port wing folded up to the top one, touching at the wing-tip. I was still apparently under some sort of control and was gliding towards the field when the top wing could not take the strain and 'gave' at the centre section, folding upwards, whereupon we fell into the ground from fifty to a hundred feet. One of the interplane struts was never found and is probably nestling at the top of one of the local trees to this day!

Reaching Dover I found I was the first member of the new squadron that had not yet been formed. Later airmen arrived and an Adjutant—Erskine Bolst—and by degrees, two more Flight Commanders, Bailey and Pearson, and we slowly collected B.E.2Cs and pupils to train on them. After a couple of months we took the then complete squadron up to Sedgeford in Norfolk, and I handed over the command to a Major Nicol. After a further month or two converting the pupils to fly D.H.9s, the bombers which they took to France, I was posted away to form and command a new Flying Instructors' School, of the same system as, and the first competitor to, Gosport.

Before leaving No. 110 I had some very entertaining times with a training aircraft, the D.H.6, known as the 'Clutching Hand' because of the exaggerated camber of its wings which, while making it very safe to fly, rendered it useless as a trainer because it gave a pupil false confidence which he rapidly lost, sometimes fatally, when going on to a more normal type. It was very slow and I had great fun in the evenings going out—with the permission of the local farmers—round the countryside shooting game with a 12-bore shotgun from the air. One had to go flat out to overtake a hare! And then, just as I or a selected pupil, Waugh or Vane Hunt, was about to fire, it would jink away and the chase continued. Pheasants and partridges were too easy, as they would allow one to fly in formation with them, and, remembering to shoot behind instead of in front, down they would go. I made a rule never to shoot anything that we could not literally bag, so we drove the game over grassland suitable for landing. Frequently I collected about six head of assorted game, all very welcome in those rationed days, for the various messes and friends and relations!

We had a Smoking Concert one night in the Officers' Mess—when smoke wasn't the only thing consumed! Captain Bailey was running it and wanted to call on Captain Kesterton for a song. There was no programme, but all were expected to do something if called upon, so Bailey said, 'I call on Keperton Castin—I mean Capsterton Kest—Keptin Casterton . . . Oh, you there! Sing!'

I started off the Special Instructors' Flight at Shoreham with some excellent instructors who had, of course, been through the Gosport course as we carried on in exactly the same manner. Frank Courtney was one, a brilliant pilot with a wonderful reputation as an aerobatic demonstrator and test-pilot. G. H. Martingell started a long association with me here, as we were subsequently together at six different stations. He was known as Martinsyde, after the aeroplane firm of that name. The four P's—Park, Pitt, Petty the Adjutant, Pensotti the Equipment Officer—C. L. Adamson and F. H. Laurence completed our staff before we grew into the larger South-Eastern Area Flying Instructors' School.

We adopted as our school marking a striped nose obtained by scratching off the black painted cowlings in four-inch wide stripes so that black and white alternated. These striped noses became quite well known particularly as none of us would arrive anywhere without a little swank—a 'falling leaf' (which I invented myself there more or less by accident) and a 'dead stick' landing up to the shed door, that is with the engine switched off and so ready to be wheeled in. Showing off, no doubt, but good advertisement for the school.

On one occasion after landing in this manner an American airman said, 'Say, Captain, did it die or did you kill it?' He meant, had I had an engine failure or did I stop it deliberately or so I assumed in time to reply, 'Oh! I killed it,' at which he appeared quite satisfied.

We worked hard all day with our many instructor pupils,

but often Courtney, Martingell and I would fly off after tea just for the fun and glory of flying in the calm of an early summer evening.

We would fly, up to half a mile apart in our three Avros, scouring the countryside for a country house with parkland or large lawn, when the spotter would have a 'forced landing'. The other two, seeing him go down, would also land to render aid. If no interesting people came out we would assume the 'fault' was put right and take off again but, if some charming daughters came to enquire, then the trouble might take some time to find and correct! It was all very good fun and, quite incidentally, good training for real forced landings.

Martingell was with me on one occasion flying from Eastchurch—where we had been examining their instructors—to Shoreham, when there was a loud bang from the engine and a complete cylinder blew off, through the cowling into space. With a rotary engine this caused a terrifying unbalance, shaking the aircraft, so the first thing necessary was to stop the engine and propeller rotating. This I managed, by stalling the Avro and then gliding in to a field before the aircraft shook itself to pieces. While waiting for a party to come out in response to our telephone call, the two of us completely dismantled the wings and had it ready to tow away on its own wheels—with the four planes and all the struts and wires neatly stacked alongside—all achieved with a bicycle kit borrowed from a girl spectator.

Only a few weeks later over Lancing College near Shoreham the same thing occurred. In a calm, matter-of-fact voice I was able to say to my pupil, 'I'll take over now; you will see that a cylinder has blown off; the first thing to do is . . .' After landing in a field he asked, 'Do you always do this? Is it part of the course? You went through the patter just as though it was a regular thing. I was most impressed.'

A periodical duty was visiting other training establishments to test flying instructors and check their methods. If not up to date, they were sent to our S.E.A.F.I.S. at Shoreham for a three-week course. On one such visit, I flew a Sopwith Pup—a little single-seater—accompanied by Captain R. H. Hawkins (now Canon Hawkins) taking a passenger in an Avro 504 two-seater trainer, from Shoreham to Witney, about ten miles west of Oxford.

I was flying in formation with the Avro because the Pup had a throttle and could therefore vary its speed, whereas with the Avro it was 'go or stop'! (The Monosoupape Gnôme engine had no throttle other than a mixture control and a switch which only permitted 'full out' or 'off'.)

On the way, thick cloud, which completely covered the sky, gradually came lower, forcing us down to keep below. We had no blind-flying instruments in those days, and when in cloud it was only the increase and decrease in noise that gave an indication of diving or climbing, or wind on the side of the face if one was side-slipping—either banked or flat. There was a kind of spirit-level bubble which was of very little use. None of this mattered very seriously if the cloud base was reasonably high, as one could fall out of cloud in a spin and have sufficient height to effect a recovery but it was just asking for trouble if the cloud base was near the ground.

We persevered, hoping to reach Witney before the clouds got too low, but were still some twenty miles from our destination when clouds and the tree-tops met. There was now danger of a collision with the other aeroplane which disappeared in the murk, so I turned to the left—on which side I had been flying—and had a hectic few minutes which seemed, at the time, interminable.

I realised that I had to get on to the ground as there was 'no future' in the air. Below tree-top height, I started a hair-raising sequence of dodging, trying to stop, and hastily restarting. A stone wall appeared and expecting a field the other side, I banged off the throttle, but before I could land the other side trees suddenly loomed up in front and I had to open the throttle and turn. But with the aircraft having lost speed, the turn was sluggish and I only scraped past the branches. Another wall appeared, back came my throttle again and when almost on the ground, another wall came in sight and I had to go on again. I tried flying at half throttle, to slow up to permit landing at short notice, but then the aeroplane was too sluggish on the controls to dodge the trees quickly enough. So I was forced to career round the countryside at full speed about twenty feet up, turning left and right in hair-raising banks missing trees by only a few feet.

Again and again I passed a suitable field and endeavoured to fly in a circle to come back to it to land, but again and again I was frustrated by the everlasting trees. Finally, I closed my throttle yet once again and managed to land on to a grass field stopping two yards from the stone wall at the unseen far end. Seldom have I known terra firma so firm and so welcome! With a huge sigh of relief I climbed out into a silent, enclosed world, unable to see more than about 100 yards.

After a short time I heard a horse approaching and, on climbing the wall, found a man ploughing the adjacent field. He was amazed to see me in flying helmet with goggles on top of my head and leather coat, not having seen my arrival.

Waiting by that road, I was lucky to stop a Service lorry full of airmen who, in due course, started me up when the clouds lifted a little, and enabled me to reach an aerodrome near Cirencester. Later still, the clouds having gone up to nearly 1,000 feet, I took off for Witney intending to search en route for the Avro. To my delight, I found it on the lawn of a big house where Hawkins had scraped in over some trees, never seeing the house. We waved to each other and he joined me successfully later at Witney.

We worked for more than a year in these schools turning out a course of instructors every three weeks and doing a great deal of flying—mostly in Avros, but also in Bristol Scouts and Monoplanes, Sopwith Pups, Camels and Snipes, S.E.5s and others, to keep our hands in. During this period we had no serious accident involving personal injury with one slight exception.

A pupil instructor was to fly an Avro solo. As the aircraft had just landed and was reported fully serviceable, he did not bother with the ground check on his engine, running it up with chocks before the wheels to prevent it moving. An airman, assuming he was going through the usual procedure, added his weight across the back of the fuselage to keep the tailplane down from the slip-stream of the propeller. The pilot, however, opened up his engine and took off straight away with the airman hanging over the rear fuselage clutching at the tailplane strut.

Weighted at the tail, the Avro left the ground and climbed steeply, in spite of the pilot frantically pushing the control column right forward. Thoroughly alarmed, the pilot looked back to see an even more alarmed face looking at him. He shut off his engine to come down, but this made the nose rise even higher and the aeroplane to lose speed and stall. He was forced to put the engine on again to prevent a spin—only to start climbing again. Desperate to get down—he did a circuit of the aerodrome, followed by the ambulance beneath, and came round to face the direction of landing over the River Adur. Again he shut off the engine to get a sequence of—nose up—stall—engine on to steady—climb—engine off—nose up—stall—engine on to steady—climb—engine off—nose up—stall, broken finally by a flat spin from which he fell flat into soft mud at the side of the tidal river. The airman, landing on his feet unhurt, squelched up to assist the pilot who had broken a wrist by gripping too rigidly the cockpit's sides to absorb the landing shock.

5

Period of peace

The Armistice came while we were at Shoreham and fairly soon after the school was disbanded and I was awarded one of the first dozen of A.F.C.s gazetted.

I was one of a small number detailed to go to France to collect some German aeroplanes being handed over as reparations under the Armistice terms. I duly collected a Fokker D.VII fighter which I very thoroughly inspected before getting airborne, as I suspected the German airmen might very well have sabotaged some part. One had fallen to bits shortly after getting into the air, only a short time previously, killing A. D. Carter who had shot down 31 German aircraft.

As I ran up the engine I noticed a German holding down the tail in the usual way with the exception that there was a large sheet of tarpaulin over him—and the tail—to protect him against the very cold wind. Instead of taking off, therefore, I got out of the cockpit and went and gave the tail a thorough re-examination to the amusement of the German mechanic who fully appreciated why I was doing it! However, all appeared sound, and I took off guessing at the labels such as 'Zu' and 'Hauptank'.

It was winter and there were many snow showers on my way to Marquise where I decided to re-fuel before crossing the Channel. I found that the compass was very obviously tampered with and was unbelievably inaccurate—something like 100 degrees out of true!

Crossing the Channel under low snow clouds as the dusk

gathered, it took all my will-power to do so on a compass course of roughly south-west when the direction was north. However, the white cliffs of Dover duly appeared as dark grey in the right place in the poor visibility and I was relieved to land at Lympne just as it was dark.

Leslie Foot of old Gosport days was there, having also brought a Fokker D.VII shortly before. We decided it would be a pity to deliver our two aircraft direct to Hounslow before we had shown them to our friends at Shoreham and Gosport so, the following morning, we set off in our Fokkers along the south coast. Over Brighton, at about 500 feet, my engine cut and I had no time to do anything but choose a landing spot, and duly came down on the golf course, immediately behind the town. Landing on a fairway my wheels trickled to a stop (no brakes, of course, then) in a small ditch and the aircraft just tipped up on its nose, balanced on the wheels and tip of propeller—which fortunately stopped vertically. Girls came rushing from a school to see what had happened, but on seeing the German black crosses on the wings and fuselage, screamed, and ran back again!

With the help of a few men we pulled the tail down and the aeroplane clear of the ditch, I was able to straighten out a slightly bent propeller tip and all was ready for take-off after more petrol had been brought from Shoreham. The men at Lympne—not understanding the German signs—had not filled the main tank, although they had chalked on the cowling 'Full P.O.W.' (Petrol, Oil, Water) which I had accepted. Only a few minutes' flight took me back to my old friends at Shoreham where I was able to show-off very satisfactorily.

Gilbert Martingell and I were both posted to Croydon to No. 24 Squadron, where we put repatriated prisoners of war through a refresher and modernising course of flying. This was a very interesting and not over-worked job, as these P.O.W.s were treated kindly with a long week-end off every week, from which we instructors benefited as well. To sit back and listen to their experiences in our private house mess in the evenings was enthralling.

During this period H.R.H. Prince Albert (later Duke of York

and King George VI) came to Croydon to learn to fly, his instructor being Captain Alec Coryton, and soon the Prince of Wales joined in, under Major Bird who, however, was posted away and I had the honour and good fortune to take his place.

The Prince of Wales was a natural flyer and could handle an Avro very well. He soon got bored with 'straight and level' and landing, and would say, 'Will you do some aerobatics?' I'd put him through the gamut of that period, loops, rolls, falling leaf and spins, giving the 'Gosport patter' all the time to show the why and the wherefore.

The first time I took off with the Prince I did so straight away from the hangar across wind which we always did, being 'Gosport'. We disdained to taxi and always landed right up to the line of aircraft outside the hangar, regardless of the wind. On this take-off I had to dip my wing to windward so that the bamboo wing skid scraped the ground. When we returned the equerry reprovingly said, 'That was a very dangerous take-off, your wing actually touched the ground!' I replied, 'Of course. It would have been dangerous if it had not done so.' He continued, 'But you should have taken off into wind, and taken much greater care with such a passenger.' I gave him the somewhat smug answer, 'I cannot take greater care of anyone than I always do; I take 100 per cent care of A.C.2 Plonk and can't do more than 100 per cent with *anyone*!' The Prince loved it.

One week-end at Hounslow he flew with Major Barker and the *Daily Mirror* next day had headlines 'Prince of Wales stunts with one-armed V.C.'. Barker wasn't one-armed, but he had very little use out of his left arm as he was still suffering from wounds in his magnificent fight against heavy odds for which he was awarded the Victoria Cross. He was able to hook his arm more or less to the throttle and managed to fly well in this manner. When the Prince of Wales came down to Croydon next day with his brother he said, 'I'm afraid I'm not allowed to fly any more; the Old Man had me up on the mat and said I had disobeyed his instructions that I was only to fly with my official instructor.' So that, unfortunately, came to a stop.

Another interesting passenger at this time was Winston

Churchill, who was then both Minister for War and Air Minister; being the sort of man he was, he thought that in order to know more about the latter post he should learn to fly. At Croydon he was given instruction by the C.O., Major Jack Scott. The Major, one of the finest men in the Service, had done great work in France during the war, but he was not the finest pilot. He had broken both legs in a crash and walked painfully with a stick.

One day he made such a bad landing with his distinguished pupil that the undercarriage collapsed and the front portion of the Avro was seriously damaged. The poor Major, in the front seat, broke both legs again, while Winston Churchill was unhurt, apart from a severe jolting and shock and to his great credit addressed the Commons that same afternoon! Jack Scott later came out of hospital and this time walked without a stick. Unfortunately he died soon after of influenza.

Winston Churchill had a beautiful farmhouse near West Grinstead and I flew him there one afternoon, landing in a field nearby where we were met by his car. I accompanied him to the house where Mrs. Churchill and her children welcomed me. A delightful tea followed in a south-west corner room from which the two outer walls had been removed to make an indoor room that was open to the garden. Tea was followed by a large whisky and a walk round the farm outbuildings which Winston was heartbroken at having to leave, saying he could not afford that as well as a town house. Also present at tea was General Sir Ian Hamilton who did, in fact, purchase the property.

I was driven back to the field where I had to teach the chauffeur how to swing the propeller without getting his head cut off. After a number of 'dummy runs' before switching on. we managed to start with no regrettable incident, and I flew back to Croydon after a very pleasant interlude.

Some years later the first Labour Government came into power and Brigadier Thompson was the first Labour Air Minister. He was raised to the peerage and thought it would be a compliment to the Service if he took the name of a Royal Air Force station in his title. He sent the list of the R.A.F. stations in to 'Boom' Trenchard, who was Chief of the Air Staff, asking him to put a tick against the name of any one advised. Trenchard, who neither approved of that Government nor its Air Minister, returned the list with two ticks against FOWLMERE and CATTEWATER. The Brigadier, in fact, became Lord Thompson of Cardington—after the airship base near Bedford.

In October 1920 I went to the Flying Wing of Cranwell to instruct cadets in the newly formed R.A.F. College at which the first-term pupils had already started. There I saw the birth of the new peace-time Royal Air Force and the training of its future leaders. I had 'B' Flight, still with the good old Avro 504Ks and towards the end of my time with Bristol Fighters and D.H.9s.

The Commandant was Air Commodore Charles A. H. Longcroft of pre-war R.F.C. fame, and commanding the Flying Wing was Wing Commander L. W. B. Rees, V.C., a great character with a fine war record. At that time the Boys' Wing was also there under Wing Commander J. Kilner—later it moved to Halton—and Squadron Leader Portal (Chief of the Air Staff in the Second World War) was Chief Instructor Flying. I had very many interesting and excellent cadets through my hands, including a future Marshal of the Royal Air Force and many others who attained very high rank and fame.

Each year I represented Cranwell at the annual R.A.F. Pageant at Hendon in the 'Avro Race', 'Relay Race', 'landing on the mark' and photography of a small ground target, in turn. We competed with each other to be the representative and my best 'line shoot' result was in the landing on the mark test. Each pilot had to climb to 2,000 feet with an observer in the back seat to see that no use was made of the engine when descending from that height to land and run up to the circle (in the middle of the aerodrome) in the centre of which was a small white mark. The idea was to be as near as possible to the mark with the centre of the undercarriage axle where the front skid crossed it. We had no wheel brakes then, of course.

My predecessor, on one occasion, went gliding down and we

watched while he ran up to the circle and came to a stop obviously plumb in the centre. The Senior N.C.O. occupying my back seat said, 'You'll never beat that, sir, he's right in the middle.' However, I shut off my engine and glided down with turns and side slips to bring me to the desired spot. We ran up to the circle, trickled into it, and came to a stop as near dead centre as could be managed. The exact measurement for my predecessor was 15 inches, and mine came to 9 inches only; I just pipped him by 6 inches, from 2,000 feet. The event was cancelled at subsequent Pageants so I was not able to try my luck against all comers.

While at Cranwell I married, in 1921, and one of my most treasured wedding presents was—and still is—a silver salver from nine members of the S.E. Area Flying Instructors' School, with a beautiful engraving of my old Avro, even to the right serial number B4391, striped nose and all correct. A present is usual from one's existing station, but one from members of a unit disbanded three years previously was unique.

6

Insurrection in Iraq

After just under two years of married life I started my long list of 'desertions' of my wife, on posting to No. 30 Squadron in Iraq in September 1923. Several others from Cranwell, including Martingell, also set out in the same small trooper, the S.S. *Glengorm Castle*. I shared a cabin for two with 'Fifi' Farrington and J. J. Williamson, sleeping on the settee under the port-hole, having lost the toss for one of the two bunks, but it was long enough and quite comfortable.

The ship of 7,000 tons was built to carry 800 people—we had 1,500 aboard! Below decks conditions were shocking, hammocks being hung three and even four deep above each other from the stanchions. Going round as Duty Flight Lieutenant at night was awful; we had to crawl under the bottom hammocks and the smell in the overcrowded, overheated space was nauseating, especially if anyone had been seasick, and the outside temperature—in the Red Sea, for instance—was up in the 100s. We eventually managed to get permission for the men to sling hammocks on decks.

In our little six feet by two feet cabin floor space we had to take it in turns to change into mess kit for dinner and dress in the morning. This was before the days of air-conditioning or even blowers in cabins. In the Suez Canal and going down the Red Sea with what wind there was behind us, the 'scoops' slung out of the port-holes did not scoop anything in at all, yet we still changed into white mess kit every night, with stiff collars. They *were* stiff to start with, but soon became quite limp, whereupon we would go and put another on and leave the limp one between the pages of a book or sheets of card-board under the mattress for use on the morrow.

After four long weeks of interminable 'Housey-Housey' (Bingo) going on the forward well-deck we reached Karachi, where the India contingent disembarked. The rest of us stayed aboard to proceed next day for another hot week up the Persian Gulf to Basra. A further crowded, hot journey for 300 miles of slow railway, finally brought us to Baghdad, where we all arrived covered with sand-fly bites and itching mercilessly. The sand-flies delighted to find some fresh blood, and with the temperature still about 110 degrees Fahrenheit we all felt 'nowt about' the country.

It was an extremely interesting time to be there. as the country had just been 'handed over' to the R.A.F. to control, and it was the first experiment of the 'Control of Under-developed Countries' by that Service instead of the Army. It was soon proved to be possible, practical and far more economical for this to be done by comparatively few aircraft instead of a considerable number of ground troops. Where it would be a week or more for a column of troops to cross the mountains to some recalcitrant village—always in risk of ambush or sniping—it would take only an hour or two for a few aero-planes to do the same thing in far greater safety. A bomb or two warning with messages dropped produced the same results without casualties on either side. Bombs would only be dropped after a warning to the occupants of the village to leave. No. 30 Squadron had a base section at Hinaidi just out-side Baghdad and forward operational detachments up at Kirkuk on the borders of Kurdistan where the trouble was at that period of time. The C.O. was Squadron Leader E. H. Johnson, a South African, and the Flight Commanders Eric Routh, and 'Sam' Kinkead, D.S.O., D.S.C., D.F.C., who was also with me at Cranwell in the previous year, and who was, unfortunately, killed in 1928 testing a Gloster Biplane float-plane for the Schneider Trophy.

When Johnson finished his time with the Squadron in January 1924, James Robb came in his place on promotion from No. 6 Squadron which was based adjacent to No. 30 Squadron at Hinaidi. Hangars and all squadron buildings were along the two sides of a large square aerodrome, with Nos. 30, 6, 8 and 1 Squadrons adjoining on the north side and round the corner on the west were Nos. 45 and 70 Bomber Transport Squadrons and the Aircraft Depot.

The squadron areas were separated by irrigation ditches in varying widths of up to eight feet and some three or four feet deep. These provided a home for thousands of noisy frogs with their assorted croaks and whistles.

Air Vice-Marshal Jack Salmond was the A.O.C. in Iraq with all troops under his command, although the Army was cut very considerably, usually to one British battalion and two Indian battalions with British officers. Also the Arab army was growing in size and experience, again with British help. They were started by the new King Feisal who had been installed by the League of Nations soon after the war had finished.

Kirkuk was about 150 miles north of Baghdad at the end of a vast plain and at the foothills of the mountainous country of Kurdistan. I was fortunate in spending nearly all my 2¼ years up here for it was 1,000 feet higher than Baghdad and consequently a degree or two cooler in the hot weather. We had a small aerodrome with a few native-built buildings; quite good, being of stone, though small. We were a very happy collection of officers, N.C.O.s and airmen who all got on well together. This was for the usual reason, that there was plenty of work to do.

We flew the ageing two-seater D.H.9As with their equally ageing Liberty engines of 400 h.p. built in American factories during the war to do 100 hours' flying. Most of our engines had completed more than four times that figure and were still going, due to the stout efforts of our excellent fitters. Work on the aircraft had to be carried out in the open with no shade—until later on one hangar was built to permit a certain amount of work under cover.

During the hot weather I saw a fitter drop a spanner from the top of the engine and it lay on the sun-drenched stones only a few minutes before he climbed down to collect it—whereupon he dropped it again with a cry and four blisters quickly came up on his fingers.

Apart from the elements, at that time we had two human enemies. Sheik Mahmoud (S.M.) was quite a good type; a Kurd patriot, who wanted Kurdistan for the Kurds. He cared nothing about any League of Nations who said, from a far-off country, that his was to be part of Iraq (itself a new name) under King Feisal (also new). He didn't want to fight the British and we didn't want to fight him, but we had to carry out our duty and did, in fact, fight him in quite a friendly way! The second enemy was quite a different cup of tea: Kerim Fatah Beg (K.F.B.) was purely and simply an outlaw and was 'agin everybody'.

K.F.B. and his followers were magnificent horsemen and would raid a village, kill and steal and be thirty miles away over mountain tracks before word could reach us or the police, about twelve hours later. Eventually we had to drop messages on all villages to say that we would destroy any village—by bombing—that supplied K.F.B. with shelter, or food for his followers and their horses. The luckless villagers were placed in a difficult position as K.F.B. in turn would threaten to pillage their villages if they withheld supplies. But our method did pay off as the villagers hid their grain and K.F.B. was kept under control.

With Sheik Mahmoud's villages—and town of Sulaimaniyah—and with those who would not pay their taxes to the British Administrative Officer, we had to drop warning messages from the air saying that if their head man did not come in by such and such a date to pay what he owed or do what he was told, we would destroy his village. Usually this was ignored, so after the necessary time had expired, back we would go and drop messages saying we would bomb the village in thirty minutes.

Those 30-minute periods were the longest half-hours I have ever known, flying around over very mountainous country watching the hardly welcoming villagers removing goats, chickens, furniture and other belongings from their mud houses and then standing aside two or three hundred yards away to watch the bombing. They accepted we would not bomb or fire at them because we had said so.

Then we dropped high explosive bombs on the village to break up the roofs and expose the timber underneath the mud covering, and then showered small incendiaries into them to catch afire the rafters and the wood inside the huts. Village after village was destroyed like this until they gave up. I took part in exactly fifty of these bombing raids, and others in the Squadron built the total up to many more.

These raids were all carried out in tired, single-engined aircraft, over many ranges of mountains of up to nine thousand feet where landings were usually impossible. On the ground, in the event of a forced landing or more probable crash, reception parties had very sharp knives which in the case of K.F.B.'s followers would certainly be used, instead of reading the 'Blood Chit' that we all carried in all local languages saying a big reward would be paid to any bringing the airmen in safely.

A long valley beyond the mountains was headed by the small town of Halebja, not far from the Persian border, which was ruled—and ruled is a very accurate word—by a famous and unusual character, the Queen of Halebja. She was very pro-British. She had a very small landing-ground close to the town and it was most interesting and rewarding to take the Political Officer, one Chapman, on his periodical visits.

The Queen was old, particularly for that part of the world where few women reached their sixties, and she was said to be over seventy. She had black hair, almost certainly dyed, and had ruled the neighbourhood since the death of her husband many years before. She was bravely pro-British and ignored both Sheik Mahmoud and Kerim Fatah Beg although the latter was only some twenty miles or so up the same valley.

It was a pleasant experience when we visited her after arriving on her very small landing-ground. She was most hospitable and meals were of the standard pattern, sitting round on the ground with a whole sheep in the centre surrounded by all sorts of local vegetables—'ladies' fingers', brinjals, etc., into which one had to dive, with no cutlery, using the right hand only—to pull off any accessible chunk, with an occasional rinse of the fingers under a long-spouted silver jug brought round by an attendant.

The most difficult meal I had in this fashion was after a few of us had spent the night there and breakfast was brought to us in our room—fortunately. It consisted of a large bowl of sizzling goat's fat in which floated fried eggs, and to tackle them with no spoon, fork or other implement presented quite a problem. Luckily chapattis were also supplied. These are the nearest thing they have to bread, resembling pancakes, so, with two of them folded up we were able to scoop out an egg and shovel all together into the mouth!

I did have a forced landing one day while setting out on a bombing sortie. Luckily it was over the foothills only about 15–20 miles from Kirkuk, but nevertheless rough and rising country. We were at about 800 feet over the hills when my engine cut completely and suddenly. My first thought was to get rid of the bombs as I considered a crash inevitable. I had a 500 lb H.E. (high explosive) bomb and one or two containers of small incendiaries. I sang out to my passenger, Flight Sergeant Wyatt, to dump them immediately and they duly went off with a great bang not far below as I approached a ridge, which I cleared with not much to spare. On looking into the small valley then brought into view, I was delighted to see a small nearly level space close to a track into which I managed to side-slip down and land successfully.

The rest of the Flight, seeing me safely down, went on to carry out the bombing mission, and about an hour or so later came back overhead, dropping a message as they went by to say, 'Well done, will send help.' A long wait ensued while armoured cars and mechanics groped their way out from No. 4 Armoured Car Company (R.A.F.) and the Squadron. During this time some locals turned up but luckily they were 'friendly' and accepted cigarettes as a token of peace. By the time the rescue party arrived we had found the cause of the trouble so, leaving a party behind with a tent and rations, I returned in one of the cars to collect the necessary spares and rejoined the aircraft the following morning.

The problem then was getting into the air again, from the

small saucer-like depression. Deciding I could do so if the aeroplane was lightened sufficiently we emptied out gallons of petrol, leaving only enough for fifteen minutes' flying. We took off the spare wheel, removed the fixed Vickers gun and the observer's Lewis gun with all the ammunition, the five-gallon drum of emergency water, the emergency rations and tool kit, and all stowed items were removed. Without a passenger I felt I could taxi as far up the side of the 'saucer' as possible and, charging down the slope along a pathway cleared of stones, that I would be able to get airborne and climb over the opposite rim.

Having run up the engine and found it satisfactory I proceeded to put this scheme into practice, when my Sergeant Fitter, Cadman by name—to his eternal credit, said: 'Are you determined to try this by yourself, sir. Because I would like to come with you.' This was absolutely unnecessary and was a splendid thing on his part. He did so purely to give me greater confidence, so I said, 'By Jove! So you shall, and we'll sail out of here without a doubt!' Perhaps the fact that he weighed about nine stone and not 15 may have affected the decision! The armoured car officer 'Simposh' Simpson and the one from the Squadron, Beaumont, went unostentatiously forward to where they thought I was bound to hit the hill opposite, but because of our lightened load we left the ground and sailed triumphantly over their heads and back to Kirkuk.

Since commercialised and famous for its oil wells from which pipe-lines run across the desert to the Mediterranean, Kirkuk then was a small town. Full of history, it was said to be the burial-place of Daniel with nearby the site of the 'Burning Fiery Furnace'. The neighbourhood was obviously over oil and a small well was worked by a family, close to the surface where goat-skins of crude oil were filled all day, and carried by donkey to an elementary refinery. This was a mud-covered mound with a fire below and the oil above refined to a parafine state. This we bought and used for our camp cooking satisfactorily.

The area smelt of sulphur and the Burning Fiery Furnace still burned—and had done so for ever, according to local legend. It was an area of approximately twenty feet in diameter, throughout which little flames were burning about eight inches to a foot high. I have walked through myself, taking care to dodge the jets of flame—as did Shadrach, Meshek and Abednego—only not having it heated up seventy-times-seven! This could be done by making more holes with a pick, but apparently, even then, they managed to get through safely!

The country around had much game and we improved our rations with sand grouse—which flew over in flocks of a million or more—snipe, occasional black-cock and duck of all sorts. Greater Bustard made good eating and sometimes fed twelve for two good meals.

We had a number of horses and 'Freddy' Guest and I shared one—though I had much more of the share than he. He later rose to high rank and distinction.

I shared a room with our Armament Officer, Frank Brockman, who was a first-rate impresario and ran very good concert-parties both at Kirkuk and Hinaidi. The party was known as 'The Palmists', so called because the squadron crest was a palm tree. I joined in with him when possible and we considered we gave much pleasure to many—chiefly, no doubt, to ourselves.

Brockers, as he was usually known, was a Gilbert and Sullivan enthusiast, and had a G & S calendar with a tear-off quotation for every day. At first rising in the morning he would tear off yesterday's date, read today's, and burst into song: 'Take a pair of sparkling eyes' or whatever it was!

We had a number of dogs and I took one of a litter early in my tour, and as he was a chotah (little) chap he took on that name, and though he grew large for a wire-haired terrier, he was the best of companions and gave me great pleasure—utterly faithful and obedient, quite fearless—he often tackled jackals and pi-dogs, much bigger than himself, and also wild cats.

My chief recollections of this time are of flying, of which we did a great deal. I did over 600 hours which is quite good going when flights seldom exceeded two hours in length and the majority about one only. The magnificence and grandeur of the scenery overcame, for me, the ever-nagging threat of an engine-failure and the almost inevitable crash that would result in attempting to land on much of the country.

Rising and falling airstreams were alarming at first though came to be expected and 'used'. When coaxing the aircraft to climb with a full load, with the engine boiling during the very hot months, a range of hills ahead would seem impossible to surmount, and a wide circle would be necessary to gain more height. Then, quite suddenly, a lift could be felt as one reached the air rising to the contour of the ground, and up the aircraft would be boosted clear of the ridge, and probably lowered down again on the far side. At times 'bumps' were very bad in these up and-down currents and two D.H.9As flying side by side might quite suddenly be separated by 500 or 1,000 feet in height and small 'bumps' which made the aeroplane feel almost out of control were occasionally the most unpleasant.

During 1924 the Arab army had its first operational experience and marched to take over Sulaimaniyah—Sheik Mahmoud's H.Q. No. 30 Squadron's aircraft had escorted the column for a week on this march, seeing it through the Bazian and Tazlujah passes, through ranges of hills where snipers could have held up an army, and they finally reached the town.

Kinkead and I, as the two Flight Commanders, thought we would do the final sortie to witness them arrive, and were in position over the town some 45 minutes beforehand. A high wind was blowing from the east over a range behind the town and sweeping down on it, which by itself would have been all right, but some ten miles to the north was a second range up to 9,000 feet—Peri Magrun Dagh. There the wind was turned in towards the town and met the other flow at right angles. The result was what was called locally a Rushobar, a good name for it in any language! The result was so remarkably unpleasant that both our passengers—Brockman was with me—were sick, and by signals Kinkead and I agreed that we would land on the small landing-ground adjacent to the town. We thought we would rather face angry humans than an angry sky.

We kept our engines running for a time in case we had to make a run for it, but had to shut down fairly soon to stop boiling. Our passengers stayed by their Lewis guns in their revolving Scarff mountings and 'Kink' and I, automatics in holsters, signed for the gathering townsfolk to sit down in a circle about 30 to 40 yards away. The notabilities of the town then appeared and virtually handed over the town to us with formalities restricted to the friendly exchanges of cigarettes. The army shortly arrived and found, to their disgust, that we had stolen their thunder.

Conditions were not always bad, of course, but flying over that country, in those aeroplanes, did provide a real challenge which was strangely exhilarating and enjoyable. There were two pilots only in the Squadron who could not face the conditions and had to be sent away.

Penny, an officer seconded from the Army for five years, being due to return to the Gunners, asked if he could fly to Sulaimaniyah and Halebja to say good-bye to friends in each place for his last trip in the R.A.F. I suppose he wanted to impress his passenger, for he flew low over a ridge on the way, and presumably met the down-draught, the wind being from the other side, for he was sucked down into the near-vertical wall of rock and both occupants were killed instantly. That was the only fatality during my time, and that should not have occurred.

Other officers in the Squadron were Langford Sainsbury, 'Monkey' Sherlock, 'Foxy' French, Jimmy Airey, Robert Edward, Bill Caster, George Wilson, 'Beery' Bashford, Cuthbert Anderson, Frank Henderson, Francis Beaumont, 'Count' Brunton, Noel Keeble (Adjutant), Jerry Atkinson, 'Dicky' Richards (Accountant), John Hawtrey, Hugh Davies, Horsey and David.

I had an interesting experience on one occasion when the rain prevented a well-known and friendly Sheik from returning over the mountains to his village of Cercian after he had been to a conference of Sheiks at Sulaimaniyah. I picked him up in my D.H.9A and packed him into the back seat with difficulty. He was a very big man—with one eye, the other always wore a black eye-shade—with the usual very baggy clothing with bandoliers of cartridges around his shoulder and waist, bristling with guns and knives of all sorts, and a voluminous turban on his head. I managed to get him to remove this (before the wind did) and to put on a helmet, goggles, and strap in before take-off. He took to it like a duck to water and I could see him taking the greatest interest in the country below that he knew so well from the back of a horse.

We had to cross two or three ridges of hills—big, steep hills—before reaching his valley, but on passing the last one, immediately a smoke fire started from his village landing-ground, some 10 miles away, to give us the wind direction for landing. They knew he was coming, and by air, but how I have no idea. There was no telephone or telegraph and the tracks were impassable due to the rain . . . but know they did. With a certain amount of trepidation I landed, wondering whether the mud would turn me over, but, though very sticky, we remained the right way up. I considered it wise not to risk a second landing so I fired off a red Very light to stop my escort doing so.

Most unfortunately I had no camera with me so missed a grand chance when Barbekr Agha stepped out. Owing to his baggy 'plus eights' he could not step over the side of the fuselage and put his foot into the two footholes, so he stood up while four of his minions made a human step-ladder for him. No. 1 stood with head bent forward—No. 2 crouched hands on knees, No. 3 on hands and knees and No. 4 lying down! It was a magnificent sight to see him, then, walk imperiously down, with the entire village forming an admiring circle round.

Shortly afterwards, an adjoining village, thinking that Barbekr Agha was still away, decided to attack his domain. They were surprised therefore to find the fierce old man very much in evidence and were duly routed and sent packing back through the dramatic gorge in the hills where the river flowed. If we had known in time we might have joined in from the air.

About this time there was a complete eclipse of the moon. We were sitting outside our mess at Kirkuk enjoying the cool of the evening when this occurred and were patronisingly amused when the locals started firing at the moon with rifles in order to kill the evil spirit that was swallowing their moon and their light. Then came a dull thud near us caused by a tired bullet falling, and there was a sly movement indoors as officers suddenly remembered that they had letters to write—or honestly said it would be a pity to get hurt or possibly even killed for such a reason!

At the time of the rain which had prevented Barbekr Agha returning to Cercian, King Feisal, still in the early stages of his rule, was held up in Kirkuk during a tour of his kingdom. 'Pa' Miller, the Administrative Officer, had to entertain him overnight and rang us up to ask if we could help. That night we happened to be giving a concert party organised by Brockman and me with members of No. 30 Squadron and No. 4 Armoured Car Company (R.A.F.) who were stationed in Kirkuk town. We said that if it would amuse His Majesty we would be honoured; so up he came, sitting in the centre of the front row with an interpreter beside him, out in the open, of course, as we had no building in which to do anything of this sort.

We had many topical jokes and words written to popular songs, which caused bursts of laughter from the audience. Somewhat to the difficulty for us on the stage who were carrying on with the performance, these jokes would be translated for the King, who suddenly gave a solo shout of laughter a minute or two later! Gradually this came to be appreciated by the audience who waited for it, and then they burst out too. So it was a sequence of joke—laughter—translation—solo laughter—general laughter. It meant the show went with a swing and we on the stage were also laughing at this sequence of events!

7

Armoured cars in Palestine

After two and a quarter years in No. 30 Squadron I was posted to 'Heliopolis Details' in Egypt in late 1925. I was delighted with this posting as I was in charge of the H.Q. Communications Flight and had an assortment of aeroplanes to fly Headquarters members round a dead-level—landable—country, and I would be able to get my wife and son out to join me, in the very good flats at Heliopolis, a suburb of Cairo.

Having received the authority for their passage, I was disgusted when, after only three weeks, my posting was changed to No. 2 Armoured Car Company in Palestine. In reply to my expostulations I was told the original posting was a mistake, as all pilots who had been flying over the mountains for two years had to be put on a ground job. So, bitterly, I went by train to Ramleh in Palestine for a complete change of life with armoured cars. After such a forbidding start I then proceeded to have two splendid years which I thoroughly enjoyed.

My dog, Chotah, was the first to join me, having been flown from Iraq (I came by sea with Christmas 1925 in the Red Sea, en route). Shortly after, my wife and two-year-old son arrived from England and we had a quarter, first at Sarafand and soon after at Ramleh. The latter was an excellent bungalow built entirely with four-gallon petrol tins filled with earth! These, with a cement wash, gave the appearance of stone. The bungalow had a double roof, tiled floor throughout, a verandah on each side of the building, two sitting rooms, three bedrooms and a bathroom. The kitchen was adjoining with quarters for the good one-eyed Ahmed who looked after us and cooked surprisingly well.

I saw all the Holy Land and much more in the following two years and had many interesting experiences with the good old Rolls-Royce armoured cars. It was then 1926 and most of the chassis were 1912, and one 1910. These had been private cars for some years, then bought during the war and had $4\frac{1}{4}$ tons of armour and extra leaves to the springs put on them. They would still do their 60 m.p.h. over a mud flat—such as was recently (1970) used for the hi-jacking of three airliners!

Although for two years my flying fever was at low temperature, fortunately No. 14 Squadron had flights stationed at Ramleh and Amman, and I was able to borrow aircraft—Bristol Fighters and D.H.9As—from them and I kept my hand in every month during this period. On one occasion in a Bristol Fighter at Ramleh, I did some 'Pilot bombing from 2,000 feet' and beat, by a good margin, the Squadron record for the average error of four practice bombs. It infuriated the Squadron that an 'armoured car wallah' should achieve this, and several members set out to get it put right . . . but they still had not done so when I left!

On another occasion—more than a year later—when we were under canvas 'out in the blue' at Kasr Azrak, one of the Squadron's Flight Commanders, Horace Wigglesworth, had a forced landing out in the lava country, and for some reason, no one from his squadron went out to him for two whole days. Feeling sorry for him, I commandeered one of their visiting D.H.9As at our landing-ground, and with another armoured car officer, Evans-Evans, in the back seat, took out a load of cigarettes, books, blankets and other provisions. We found his aeroplane on a strip cleared of lava rocks and marked out. When I landed and he saw who it was, he flung his cap on the ground in fury, 'Well, I'm . . . ! Two armoured car officers—no one from my own squadron!' He was justifiably annoyed but also grateful to us for finding out what was needed to get him airborne again, and for the comforts meantime.

At Azrak were two 'lakes' in which it was nearly pleasant to bathe at the end of a hot, sticky and dusty day—the qualification 'nearly' being caused by the mosquitoes! We had our camp about half a mile away for this reason; to bathe we would put on our trunks in our tents, get into a Rolls tender and drive to the water's edge—run and dive in. Even then much splashing was necessary before putting one's head out! After ten minutes or so of good cooling, one of us would say 'All out—Go!' Whereupon a rush would be made to the bank and so to the Rolls tender and away as quickly as possible, in a heap, without pausing to dry.

During this period some interesting months were spent on the sidelines, as it were, of the French-Druze war in Syria. The Druze, an attractive tribe, didn't approve of the French, sent by the League of Nations, in their country and did what they could to annoy. The French came to visit us in our camp at Azrak, where they couldn't believe their eyes when they saw we did not have any native women there! They told us that the Druze were in the habit of crossing over the border from Syria into Trans-Jordan (as it was then) going round in a semi-circle and re-crossing to attack the French supply lines and rear positions and could we please do something to stop it.

On several occasions we intercepted large bands of armed Druze raiding parties and bid them retrace their steps. They treated it as a big joke and duly returned without argument, acknowledging that they had been caught out—and also appreciating that four armoured cars with Vickers guns trained on them are not things with which to trifle.

We found that the old-fashioned topee was a very unsuitable headgear for use on and in armoured cars. When sitting inside the turret it caught on the door and turret and was in every way too big and a nuisance, while outside it caught the wind and scooped in the dust and was an effort to keep on.

We therefore, unofficially, adopted the Arab headgear of a kuffiyah and argal which we dyed khaki—in coffee—and this proved to be entirely satisfactory. It fitted the head and so did not take up room inside the turret, while outside it was snug to the head and did not catch the wind, had a good flap down over the neck and back to protect against the sun and, best of all, could be wound round over the nose and mouth as an air filter against the everlasting sandy dust. This portion could be tucked in under the argal and kept firmly in position. Objections were raised by 'higher authority' that we were not wearing regulation dress, but on appreciating our very sound reasons this headgear was eventually made official.

At Amman one afternoon when we had just got on to our beds in our tents—with a towel round the waist—for the afternoon 'snurge', the earth started suddenly to quake in a very frightening manner. A tent is a very good place to be in an earthquake, though we had a doubt that we might slide down the side of the wadi on which was our camp, as landslides were going on all along the steeper sides, with huge clouds of dust.

Poor Chotah—my dog—could not understand, literally, what on earth was happening. His drinking bowl, level on the ground, was slopping water over its sides. Whimpering, he came in a wobbly run over to me to find out what I could do about it. It only lasted about 30 seconds but, in that time, there were a thousand deaths in Amman and neighbouring villages, though curiously there was not a single British casualty. We were not near enough to Amman town to be of help and had to assist in the permanent brick buildings of the No. 14 Squadron aerodrome where many were badly cracked and had to be evacuated, pulled down and rebuilt.

During 1926 I had to go with my section of cars for two months 'out in the blue' with a company of Levy mounted infantry under a Captain Yard-Buller. Here we guarded our frontier which I had also to delineate. We spent days and nights sleeping by the cars, marking the undefined frontier on the north. This we did after consulting maps and compass, by building cairns of stones on the highest bits of the undulating country and painting them white so that each was visible from those on each side. One such spot appears on the later Survey map as 'Vincent's Cairn'!

With regular flag-waving trips from the extreme north of Palestine down through Tiberias, with bathing in the Sea of Galilee, Nazareth, Jerusalem of course, Jericho, the Dead Sea (very unpleasant bathing here in the steamy-oven salt sea at 1,200 feet below sea-level), Jaffa, sea-bathing in the Mediterranean (Joppa of the Bible). Then across the muddy brown Jordan, up the steep hill to Es Salt and Amman, we saw more of the country at close quarters than could be seen by normal squadron service.

One patrol took us right across to Baghdad entailing hot, very dusty and sweaty times in loose sand and in lava country, involving clearing tracks through large black boulders, slowing us to less than a mile on one day. However, with an excellent bunch of airmen, we got on very well and I had to admit that it was all a wonderful experience, and given only to a few.

A riot started in Jaffa over some political squabble one day, and I was sent with my section of cars to quell it. I asked Group Captain Rees, the Senior British Officer who had been my Wing Commander at Cranwell, if I had to fire to stop the trouble, whether I should fire over their heads, or shoot to kill? He replied, 'Vincent, that can only be decided by the man on the spot, but I assure you that whichever you do, you will certainly be court-martialled'! Fortunately our threat was sufficient.

Early in 1928 I left No. 2 Armoured Car Company to return home, but with a lump in my throat at leaving my much-loved dog, whom I had passed on to a newcomer in the Company, Cyril Greet, who was obviously genuinely fond of him. He had been with me for over four years and had adopted my wife and small boy to whom he became almost a nurse. However, back I went and was posted to No. 1 Squadron at Tangmere, where I returned once more to a single-seater fighter, the Armstrong Siddeley Siskin.

8

Squadron Commander

Tangmere was an extremely pleasant station, near Chichester and the South Coast—and Goodwood Golf Course. It was a sunny part of England and often had beautiful clear weather while the rest of the country, just across the South Downs, was under low cloud. Taking full advantage of this we were able to do a lot of flying. We had a new married quarter and pleasant neighbours so life was good.

On days when there were large banks of cumulus clouds we played a game, in 'A' Flight, of follow-my-leader, round, over, under and through valleys but never actually inside the cloud. The idea was for the leader to lose his followers; it really did teach quick reactions necessary for a fighter pilot. The leader would dive through a gap and promptly climb vertically up beyond the cloud, over the top and a diving turn after and so on. It got increasingly difficult for the followers and usually No. 4 would get flung out on the whip-lash effect. Then a reformation—No. 2 would lead and No. 1 then tagged on the end and so on . . . it was exhilarating.

One of my lasting impressions of flying came from a trip at Tangmere; night-flying in a Siskin at a time when it was completely clouded over at about 2,000 feet, and very dark and dreary. I climbed up into the cloud, as by this time we had the necessary instruments and after about another 1,000 feet suddenly came out into a clear sky with an almost full moon. The effect of this sudden change was staggering; mile after mile of almost flat but dimpled white 'eiderdown' below and a dome of clear sky with myriads of stars and the moon above. I sang with joy, and it was perhaps lucky that it was pre-radio telephony so that other aircraft or ground stations could not hear. After too short a time I had to come back to murky reality by descending well to the south of the aerodrome so that I would not fly into the Downs.

Twice, during my three years there, the Squadron won the inter-squadron annual gunnery competition for which we did our air-to-ground and air-to-air (towed-target) firing at Sutton Bridge on the Wash. We spent three weeks there carrying out the various practices and competitions daily. I was the individual winner the first year and was second the following. On the last occasion we had to fly back to Tangmere on Friday the 13th with a formation of thirteen aircraft, which I led in spite of an adverse weather report and low clouds with rain showers. Several pilots were apprehensive, so I related my Friday the 13th experiences in France. By squeezing through the 'Shoreham Gap' in the Downs, we all duly arrived.

A disconcerting incident did occur when we were practising for one of the Hendon displays. With No. 43 Squadron, who shared Tangmere with us, and No. 25 Squadron from Hawkinge, we were to carry out Wing manœuvres including aerobatics of a fairly mild but showy type. One exercise entailed the Wing in line astern, diving down in succession followed by a climb into a half-loop with a half-roll off the top, so that the line snaked back over itself. This was a reasonably safe manœuvre as the climb into the half-loop would take the leader and those following well above those still diving at a fairly gentle angle, and the half-roll would take them slightly out of line to those following.

Eustace Grenfell, leading our squadron which led the whole wing, was over-anxious that when he pulled over he would be well above those down the line. So as he started his half-loop, he kept going up and up before pulling over at the top. Leading the second flight of three, I was No. 4 in line close behind No. 3 of the leading flight. When I got into the vertical position, the other two ahead were still going vertically themselves, straining to follow No. 1 and I realised that No. 1 himself would not be able to carry out his half-roll, and would be bound to lose too much speed and fall out of it to the danger of all below. No. 2, also realising this, pulled over with his half-loop, but already having lost speed did a sloppy twist; No. 3, overtaking him, hit his tail with his propeller. I could see all this happening in front of me and decided to complete my half-loop and half-roll while I had full control, so over I went, thus avoiding what was happening above.

Those behind followed me according to plan, so I found myself leading a long line of Siskins which I proceeded to re-form into squadrons by signals, and break up the party.

Grenfell, 'waffling' out of the top of his half-loop, came out at 90 degrees to that desired entirely on his own. No. 3, with a smashed propeller, was fortunately over the aerodrome and so could shut off his engine and landed successfully. No. 2, having lost part of his tailplane, contemplated taking to his parachute, but realising he could maintain level flight, climbed to a safe height for parachuting to find out if there was sufficient control to attempt landing. Finding the minimum safe speed that he could use down to ground level, he very ably brought his damaged aeroplane down to a successful landing. Grenfell then decided he would not try to lead the formation, and it fell upon 'old Joe' and I led from then on.

Tangmere was a happy time and after three years I, at last, got my promotion to Squadron Leader, after eleven years as a Captain and its equivalent Flight Lieutenant. I was posted to take over No. 41 Squadron at Northolt, also with Siskins but fairly soon converted to Bristol Bulldogs. I found the Squadron very un-fighter minded; aerobatics and formation flying were sadly neglected. I had to work hard with competitions for the former and regular days every week for the latter, until they slowly became a good squadron.

The next stage in R.A.F. sophistication evolved about this time, parachutes as regulation came during my No. 1 Squadron service. With No. 41 came Radio Telephony (R.T.)—that is, speech replaced the Morse signals of Wireless Telegraphy (W/T) used hitherto. Our sets, on medium wave bands, had to be adjusted by pilots to a high degree of sensitivity, so that conversations between air and ground and air to air was doubtful and there was considerable interference from adjacent channels and other 'noises off'. 'Taffy' Taaffe, commanding 'C' Flight, always seemed to have more difficulties than others.

On one occasion, when practising squadron formation, I said, 'Turning to port—Turning to port—Go', to hear him reply, 'Understand to switch off—switching off—off' and off the air he went, packing up the whole R/T exercise.

On another occasion the Squadron had flown to Filton for a very fine entertainment overnight by the Bristol Aeroplane Company when we had completed our re-equipment with Bulldogs. The following morning, in view of the 'night before', I deemed it wise to take off by flights instead of as a squadron and to form up overhead. Four flights duly took off and three met up overhead. I called and called to 'Firefly Blue' but got no reply, nor could 'C' Flight be seen, so finally I set course for Northolt still calling periodically to Taffy.

After a while he burst in, 'Hello! Hello! Hello! Firefly Leader, this is Firefly Blue.'

So I asked where the blazes he was and back came the reply, 'I'm over Chipping Sodbury.'

The whole of our three flights then rocked up and down as the pilots laughed, and I answered, 'You would be!' So R/T had its lighter side, and steadily improved to the Very High Frequency (V.H.F.) reliability of the Battle of Britain time, nine years later.

Trials at this period started for the control of fighters from the ground. A small Operations Room was contrived in which a controller gave instructions to the Fighter Leader by Radio Telephony through the medium of an airman operator. On one occasion the controller, trying to intercept the 'bomber', gave the order 'Patrol Halton 15,000 feet', which was passed on by a Cockney operator as 'Patrol 'Alton 15,000 feet'!

After much searching on his map, the Fighter Leader duly led his formation down to Hampshire instead of Buckinghamshire and two early lessons were learned:

1. The controller must give the orders himself
2. That place names on a map are useless

During one of our annual 'Air Defence of Great Britain' exercises No. 41 Squadron was detailed for night work for four nights. We were sorry about this, as it was always good fun by day bringing off interceptions of bomber squadrons coming in over the North Sea or English Channel and carrying out the mock standard attacks.

However, night it was ordered to be. Patrol time was split up into 90-minute periods and we went off two at a time to cover quite a wide patrol line, hoping to spot the Vickers Virginias and attack them from astern. If we intercepted, the drill was to switch on our navigation lights which the bomber acknowledged in like manner to effect a 'shot down'.

Every pilot flew at least once and some twice in the darkness period, and it was my turn on the last night to be with the first pair and also the last. I had to go to the Newbury area where, by good fortune, I was in the right spot and at the right height to be just below the bomber stream. Seeing the bombers silhouetted against the slightly lighter sky, I brought off attacks on no less than six in fairly rapid suucession, as they were only a mile or so apart.

Very pleased with myself I flew back to Northolt at the end of my time, facing the east where I then saw the most beautiful sunrise. I stayed up at my height over the aerodrome in order to get the full effect of this magnificent sight and then came down to the semi-darkness where the sunrise had not yet reached . . . and then saw it all over again, though not with the expanse of an empty sky. I feel I can still see it, and realise the privileges that flying bestows. Alas! Those wonderful times are over.

I had two years of much satisfaction barring a few rows with my 'so smug' Station Commander. 'As I was walking back from my office at 19.30 hrs last night, Vincent, I saw . . . etc., etc.,' he would say, knowing that I had left mine at 17.30 hrs, the official closing time! These rows stopped when I finally lost my temper when he tried, unjustifiably, to run my squadron as well as the station, and said, 'You don't want a Squadron Leader there—you want a bloody civilian clerk!'

At the end of my tour in April 1933 I was posted back to

Iraq once again, and at fairly short notice, as the C.O. of No. 84 Squadron had been sent home as a sick man after only two months with the Squadron. As I had missed the official trooping season I went out in much greater comfort than the first time. I travelled, with four other R.A.F. officers, in the Orient liner *Otranto*. We disembarked at Port Said and were flown over to Baghdad, and finally in a Southampton flying boat to Basra.

9

Wapiti and Vincent days

Shaibah, where No. 84 Squadron was stationed, was seventeen miles into the desert from Basra—dead flat, no road, just sandy soil, and from the station the view was dead flat as well, not a tree, bush or blade of grass to be seen in any direction. It was very different from Kirkuk, 450 miles to the north. An airman new to the Squadron, a Northerner, remarked on gazing at the view, 'Ah, it's a bit dull 'ere!'

At the station there was the Squadron, with Westland Wapiti two-seaters, a large signal section which was a wireless 'Clapham Junction' between the U.K. and the Far East. There was also the Imperial Airways staging post, hangar, office, accommodation and messing for passengers of the Handley Page Hannibals which made regular weekly stops in each direction—east and west—and there was a native village built for the coolies who worked in the camp with their wives and families, and a company of Arab Levies, with a British C.O., as guards—all in the perimter wire commanded by one Squadron Leader. Nowadays an area of this size—far bigger than the United Kingdom—would be the responsibility of at least a Group Captain with a large staff.

The climate made it impossible for wives, so we were very much an all-male population. The temperature rose every year gradually up to 125 degrees Fahrenheit in the shade, and periodically to as much as 130. For two winter months it was quite pleasant and a fire was attractive in the messes in the evenings. There was no air-conditioning and only slowly turning fans moved the hot air gently about.

In the hot months we got up at 04.00 hrs in the morning, flew and worked for two hours before breakfast and again to mid-day, when we had lunch and retired to a bed, on the metal part of which it was extremely painful to put your hand. With just a towel round the waist, a sticky time was spent until about 16.00 hrs, then a shower followed by a round of golf on the twelve-hole course which I had made (in three months), where clubs and balls could be hired from the N.A.A.F.I.—fixed with the U.K. in advance—a shower, then perhaps a game of squash (even at 110 in the shade!)—another shower and a bathe in the fire pool, possibly a game of water-polo—officers versus sergeants or corporals or airmen, when the main object appeared to be to get me, as C.O., pushed to the bottom as often as possible! One more shower, and a change into our own version of the white mess kit, white trousers, black cummerbund, white silk shirt with rank epaulettes and a black bow tie; very smart and comfortable. Then a large double whisky and iced water which was really deserved and 'out of this world'!

Cricket, hockey and even football were played for most of the year, with the result that our first football XI won the inter-station cup in my last year, and the second XI the cup for the smaller stations, which was a great occasion. We flew in squadron formation to Hinaidi (Baghdad) for the finals—and celebrations—shortly before I left for home.

Shaibah, despite its lack of amenities, was a very happy station. Everybody had to work hard both in working hours and also to make entertainment for themselves; nothing was laid on, with the result that games flourished, as did concert-parties, dances (all male), band concerts and fancy-dress costumes and decorated barrack rooms at Christmas.

I managed to get a cinema show once a week from Basra for most of the year, out of doors of course. On one occasion a Pathé News included a fashion parade. This was accompanied by suitable appreciative remarks from the all-male audience until a sudden hush when a model 'For the fuller figure' came on, until, after the suitable pause, a voice came up with: 'All right, wrap it up, I'll 'ave it'!

It was not all play as it might, so far, appear. We were

responsible for a vast area of country, about 200 miles of desert to the west and north, and about 1,500 miles or more down the Persian Gulf, where we had landing-grounds at Bahrain, Sharjah, Muscat and Masireh, which we visited regularly 'waving the flag'.

Other interesting places visited were Kuwait and Ur—that oldest city so helpful to crossword-puzzle setters. It was here that one of my predecessors in the Squadron had obtained a load of 3,000 or more years-old bricks and built them into a very attractive fireplace in the officers' mess for use on a few occasions in the short 'cold' weather period. The cuneiform writing on these bricks was decipherable to experts.

We had—for some reason which I never quite understood—Wapiti J9838 fitted with floats at Margil, which was the Basra station of No. 203 (Flying Boat) Squadron, who maintained it for us. I had never flown off the water so found this a very new and pleasant experience. It was not only amusing to take off and 'land', but it was very satisfying to come down and cleave the waters on the smooth river, and then the challenge of getting a single-engined, barely steerable aircraft on to a slipway across a fast-running stream, with the wind helping or hindering. Another interesting aircraft, at Shaibah in July 1933, was the Bristol 118 private venture general-purpose aircraft (K2873) on a tropical trials visit.

We were, as I said, an all-male community. An enterprising and unscrupulous native came and pitched several tents with women close to our wire and let it be known that they were procurable. I sent messages out to them to tell them to go—but they took no notice. I therefore took up my Wapiti and dived on a line parallel with their tents and fired my front Vickers gun about fifteen yards away from the tents. It was marvellous to see the tents being struck and packing up. They thought I was shooting at them and missing and that I might not do so next time! We saw them no more!

A little rising at Sur was quickly quelled by a formation demonstration overhead and a R.N. sloop in the Gulf. We had long-range tanks attached to our Wapitis and could remain in the air for over eight hours; this is a long time to sit in one unalterable position, unable to move the feet with any degree of comfort or 'spend a penny', especially when we were only doing about 100 m.p.h., but we frequently did the 800 miles to Sharjah in this way. The Wapiti was built in order to use up a great number of D.H.9A parts, but the fuselage was new, and with a Bristol Jupiter radial engine it was a great deal more modern and reliable than the old Liberty of the D.H.9A.

During my time the Squadron was re-equipped with Vincents which were larger, more powerful, a little faster, and could carry much greater loads. They also had brakes which made them of much greater value, landing on the little 'dumb-bell' strips of only 200 yards in length, as at Margil (Basra) which was the only connecting link in the short wet-weather period, when the desert track was impassable.

At the time of this re-equipment the Royal Air Force List used to give the names of all officers in a squadron and, as we were the first one to be equipped with this particular aeroplane, I like to think Vickers looked in the list and saw the C.O.'s name started with a V and thought they might as well use that name as well as any other!

Signals of aircraft movements were always sent out with the abbreviation of the aeroplane and name of the pilot, so I was known to Air Headquarters first as 'Wop Vincent' and finally as 'Vin Vincent'.

In 1934 the first reinforcement flight to Singapore was carried out and I managed to persuade A.H.Q. to let me lead and leave my senior Flight Commander—Rodwell—in charge at Shaibah. Four Wapitis, therefore, left Shaibah, accompanied by two Valentias under Squadron Leader Yool which were our 'luggage carriers' with various spares, although they needed so many assorted spares for themselves that not much space was left for us. Our object was to report on all landing-grounds on the way, conditions, and the general feasibility of the operation.

With our long-range tanks we flew to Sharjah for the first night, and on to Karachi in India for the second. The other three pilots were allotted by drawing lots—one Flight Lieutenant, Walter, one Flying Officer, Williams, and two Sergeant Pilots, Scrace and Christmas, the last named as a reserve. I had the only wireless operator, Colquhoun, with me in J9844, the others shared two fitters and a rigger. In stages we proceeded via Jodhpur, Allahabad, Jansi and Calcutta across India, and down into Burma and Malaya via Akyab and Rangoon, finally arriving in a formation of six over Seletar in Singapore at the time originally planned—and in time for a gin before lunch at mid-day.

One of our engines—in Williams' Wapiti—gave trouble and we had to change it here, but without extending our six days' scheduled stay. We left by the same route and duly flew over Shaibah once again in a formation of six aircraft at the scheduled time—in time for a whisky before the evening meal.

On the way out, south of Chittagong, Squadron Leader Yool had an oil pipe break in his Valentia and Colquhoun picked up his wireless message to say where he was. I went to the spot and found him safely landed on a nice little stretch of beach with the tide out. This was the only stretch of beach for 300 miles, as mangrove trees grew right into the sea from swampy jungle inland, and there would have been no possible chance of a landing a matter of minutes later. I dropped a message asking him to fire a green Very light if he was going to be able to take off again, and was relieved to see that colour light come up. Meanwhile he and his passengers were vigorously chewing gum, which was used with insulating tape to seal the severed ends of the broken pipes, before the tide came in! In the nick of time, while there was still firm sand, he took off and joined us later at Tavoy, where we remained overnight.

The good people of Tavoy took on this sudden unexpected invasion and gave us a most splendid, hospitable time. They put us all up in various houses, and arranged a party at their club. I was staying with the Senior British Representative and several of us were having a drink on his verandah after a bath and a borrowed change, when three beauteous girls, who were staying with friends, came on to the verandah and, standing together in the centre and pointing at each of us in turn, said: 'There's one, there's two, there's three, there's four, there's five —OOOOH! Wapiti, Wapiti, Wapiti!' So that set the standard for the evening! So much so, in fact, that we altered our return schedule to stay another night there, when we were again very well entertained with a moonlight picnic on the beach and a bathe.

On our return trip, when we landed at Jodhpur in long grass, we were met by four of the Maharajah's open cars and a number of beautiful twelve-bore shotguns and the request for us to shoot as many gazelles and vultures as we could, as the gazelles, hiding up in the long grass, were a menace to his private aircraft landing and taking off, while the vultures circled overhead and were also a grave risk. So we drove around in the grass and duly knocked off seven gazelles and also some vultures who were on to the corpses immediately. I achieved what I feel sure can never have been done by anyone else, by getting a left and a right on two vultures—one had a seven-foot wing span.

The Persian Gulf is about seventy miles across where we planned to fly over, and I arranged with the Senior Naval Officer Persian Gulf to have one of his sloops about half-way across as a precaution against one of our getting-a-bit-tired engines cutting out. We saw no sign of any ship and when Colquhoun gave them a call on the W/T we found they were about 500 miles north and couldn't care less what might become of us! However, the good engines gave us no worry and we came over rather lower than those following liked, because I was having trouble with a tooth and as soon as we reached 4,000 feet it jumped and stabbed, so I dropped down to a lower altitude at once. There we could see large sharks basking on the surface; as soon as they could hear us they rolled over, showing their lighter bellies and dived down. That made us give extra thanks to our steadily functioning engines.

So '4 aircraft Wop Vincent and 2 Val Yool' finished a splendid five weeks, having thoroughly enjoyed the whole experience, mostly in good weather, but with some real tropical rain in Malaya, where we had to land in a downpour into what looked like a lake at Taiping, with very bad visibility. There was enough flying to satisfy any glutton with flying fever.

Not long after this I was at Bahrain with another pilot, where we spent the night in our little rest house. This consisted of one room with four beds in a row. Presumably, we were both bitten by the same anopheles mosquito during the night as, a week or so later, back at Shaibah, we both went down with high temperatures. Although we had alternate shivering and sweating periods, the new and inexperienced doctor was convinced it was sand-fly fever, and never even gave us quinine, although I said I was sure it was malaria.

We grew steadily worse until my Senior Flight Commander, Rodwell, became alarmed and sent for a more experienced medical officer from the hospital in Margil—Basra. He saw immediately what the trouble was and ordered us into hospital at once. We travelled the seventeen miles after dark, when it was a bit cooler, in two ambulances, over the bumpy desert track—me trying to vomit but being unable to do so as I had nothing in me. I do not recommend that journey to anyone in such conditions.

We were put in two adjoining rooms and, feeling really ill myself, I heard my co-sufferer start to sing. He was a big, hefty Canadian, a boxer called Supple, and had been fit as could be before this. While the dear nurses held his hand and mopped his brow, he sang all the mess songs—like the famous 'Shaibah Blues'—and soon sang himself out of this world. I wondered if he was still singing the same songs when he arrived in the next. The malaria had gone to his brain; I imagine I had not the brain to attract it, but had a very bad week with double malaria, longing for the sleep which I was unable to get during all this time. The best of fine nurses kept ice on my head while I prattled nonsense, until at last I got over it, and was promptly sent back to England for two months' convalescence.

I started the homeward journey as a passenger in a Victoria to Ramleh in Palestine. It was very hot, the machine could not fly very high so it was bumpy, and it was full of sick airmen also leaving for health reasons, including one stretcher case. The last leg of the journey over the Judean hills was particularly bad, and an open-ended five-gallon drum stood in the centre of the fuselage, into which most of the passengers took it in turns to be sick, in front of me, and the unhappy one on the stretcher also trying to find the bowl held by the medical orderly, when he himself was not at the five-gallon drum. Not being in fine fettle myself, I was mighty glad I held out, and was not air-sick which would have been the only time in my thirty-five years in the Service.

The rest of the homeward journey by ship, train, ship and train again, saw me home, and at the end of the two months, to the surprise and almost annoyance of the Air Ministry and the medicos, I insisted on returning to Shaibah to finish off the last three months of my tour. So back by the same assorted means of transport—train, ship and aeroplane—I felt I could clear my conscience for missing the two hottest months. Even then my full time was cut short by a week or two as I was posted home in order to attend a year's armament course at Eastchurch.

I left Shaibah on the last day of January 1935 after a great send-off—but in the back of a Valentia—and escorted for the first thirty miles or so by a full squadron formation of Vincents. I was able in those last months to do a few more trips down the Persian Gulf and showed the Bahrain mosquitoes that, at least, I was still flying! Bahrain, in its pre-oil days, was a good port of call for us, as there was a beautiful pool a short distance inland, which was in rock, and crystal clear. It was at the same temperature all the year round, whatever the air temperature. One could see rocks and weeds at the bottom, apparently accessible, but these could never be touched even by the deepest divers, being probably thirty feet or more down.

Sharjah was an old fort, which we used as accommodation, feeling very 'Beau Geste' and Foreign Legion. It had small rooms round a courtyard, with a high surrounding castellated wall, and a single thick-gated entrance. There was, however, wireless communication with the outside world, and a few good airmen to service and refuel aeroplanes, and to cook and guard.

Muscat was a small landing-ground in between hills a mile or two behind the town, supposedly the hottest place in the world. I don't know if this is so, but it is certainly very hot indeed, being in black lava country, where the lava, throwing the heat back at one, is so hot that it is impossible to handle without blistering the hands. We had a small rest house down by the sea and we naturally thought that a bathe would be refreshing, but when in the sea, the wish at once was for someone to turn on the cold tap. The water was most unrefreshingly warm.

So my second Iraqi tour was very different from the first, but still full of interest and also with a great deal of flying. Then, after only one week's leave, off I went to Eastchurch in March 1936 where the change was very great—school, and (addled) brain work, and very little flying.

10

Station Commander

For two or three months I found the going very hard as I had left school twenty years before and also, coming straight from a strenuous time in a very hot climate, my brain just couldn't keep up with 'the professor' at the blackboard, doing higher maths of ballistics. But after much ice on a fevered brow at night-time trying to work out what was said in the morning, I suddenly found comprehension returning, and at the end of the course I passed out quite high.

During this year we did a certain amount of practical work—gunnery and bombing—and we were paired off to fly each other for this. I had to fly, alternating as passenger and pilot with a chap called Fear, and I certainly did fly with fear as he was not much of a pilot! In a Bristol Fighter I had to lean over and shout in his ear when to close his throttle and when to pull his stick back to land. However, I enjoyed my piloting part of two- and single-seater work.

At the end of the year's course I put in a paper to show that the Air Fighting Development Unit at Northolt ought to be commanded by a qualified Armament Officer, as so much of its work included the very problems on which we had been working on the course. It happened also, that besides being a very interesting appointment, I had a house and family two miles from that aerodrome . . . ! So, having proved that an armament type was needed, I was then able to point out that there was no one better qualified than I to fill the post. I was duly posted to this very enjoyable and worth-while job in December 1936.

I had a single-seater fighter squadron (No. 111), a two-seater fighter squadron (No. 23), and a twin-engined bomber squadron (No. 57 and later No. 101) to play with, or perhaps 'work with' would be more the case. No. 111 had Gloster Gauntlets, No. 23 Hawker Demons and No. 101 Boulton & Paul Sidestrands and later Overstrands. I had a Gloster Gladiator and a Hawker Fury II in which to accompany the formations, and with which to give any instructions or alterations to the prearranged attacks, but I also used Bulldogs, Hinds and Harts.

We worked out methods of attack and defence, and with cine-camera gun pictures could assess the results fairly satisfactorily. Types of bomber formations were found to be extremely effective—but when the war came and early daylight raids were carried out by our bombers, they went in the old-fashioned manner with consequent and immediate terrible casualties. These could have been minimised had they only used methods that we took so much time and trouble to find out.

On one occasion we had climbed through a solid layer of cloud and flew up and down a line to the west of Northolt, not realising there was a very strong westerly wind above the cloud. At the end of our time I signalled to wash out and return and dived down in my Gladiator to find quite unfamiliar country from where I had anticipated somewhere between Reading and Windsor. I flew east for a short while before realising I must be well east of London, and, turning back, eventually found out where I was when I saw Debden, where I had to land to refuel. I did this as quickly as possible and flew back to Northolt to find No. 23 Squadron just landed. Squadron Leader Eccles, their C.O., had recognised a large house with a long avenue where friends of his lived, and which he had visited! The single-seater fighters had also landed to refuel, having finally found themselves at Martlesham Heath, near Ipswich.

My promotion to Wing Commander came through after twelve months and I took over command of the station, having had the unusual and unpleasant duty of placing my Station Commander under arrest! This was not due to any 'crime' committed against me personally or the station, but was owing to a series of rather foolish verbal and written squabbles with the Air Officer Commanding Fighting Area. I was required to go to the Group Captain's married quarter early one Sunday morning and tell him he was not to leave his house. and that I would relieve him of his command of the station. I remained so until the end of 1936 when I went to Air Ministry as Training (Armament) Staff Officer in the Directorate of Training.

Groaning at my chair-borne appointment, I was delighted, after three months, when I was selected as the senior one of two R.A.F. officers to attend the Royal Naval Staff College at Greenwich, on recommendations submitted before I went to the Ministry. I managed to get in some flying while in this job, to visit training establishments in Anglesey, the Isle of Man and South Wales, where I walked many miles and selected areas which were later made into aerodromes and bombing ranges on the coast.

Though I flew few hours, I flew seven different types of aircraft during the year—but then, in those happy pre-war years one did fly very many different types. If a friend was serving in 'X' Squadron—a visit for lunch would be followed by a flight in his different type of aircraft. I, like many others, have well over a hundred different types in my log-book, which make an embracing coverage of monoplane, biplane, triplane, sesquiplane, pusher, tractor, off land and water; single-, two- and four-engined; with stationary, rotary, radial and jet engines. I can only include helicopter as with an official pilot in charge. Most of them were enjoyable in some way or another.

I have often been asked which was the nicest aeroplane I've flown; this is almost impossible to answer as aircraft are built for different purposes, but I suppose the Gloster Gauntlet was perhaps the most enjoyable. Its forerunner was sent as a Gloster F10/27 together with a Bulldog IIIA(R-5) and an Armstrong Siddeley successor to the Siskin, the A.W.16, for service trials when I had No. 41 Squadron, where we gave them very thorough testing and comparison, to choose which should succeed the Bulldog. I recommended the Gloster, provided it had the bigger engine (as in the Bulldog IIIA) and that the top plane be moved forward a few inches to counteract the added weight and to improve the visibility. *Mirabile dictu*—the Air Ministry agreed and Glosters carried out the modifications in a matter of a few months, and the Gauntlet was the result. It had no vices. was comfortable to fly, had a good performance, could do all aerobatics, was easy and slow to land, and had good visibility.

But the old Avro 504 served me for several hundred hours and I really felt I could make it 'feed out of my hand' and do anything with it, land anywhere, and even though I spent seven months in hospital after the unexplained failure of one, I have many nostalgic feelings for it.

Later, the Spitfire gave once more the feeling of being one with it—rather like the Sopwith Pup and the Camel of the first war—and was a lovely aeroplane though I did not fly it nearly as much as the Hurricane, which was different, but was a really steady war horse rather than a race horse, but also good to fly from this point of view.

During my time at the Greenwich Staff College flying was still further cut down, but I managed to fly five types on a few occasions by skilful borrowing.

And then came the war.

Having been at Greenwich and because I knew that Dr. not only stood for 'Doctor' but also 'destroyer', I was sent to the combined H.Q. at Plymouth as a Controller, where I spent four months of the phoney war telling people to do things in Sunderland flying boats and Avro Ansons, neither of which I had flown myself, and therefore disliked this work intensely.

I flew a Miles Magister, a small two-seater trainer, at Roborough on several occasions including one week-end leave when I went to the Civil Aerodrome at Wilmington near Eastbourne, where my family were staying. First thing on Monday morning in a thick fog I groped my way to this small landing-ground by taxi. There I waited until late afternoon when it cleared sufficiently for me to get back in the air. I flew westward as fast as the machine would go, but as Shoreham came in view it had darkened so I thought I would push on to my old station at Tangmere where I thought I could land without flares.

Arriving there by the knowledge of the local landmarks, I was pleased to see a flare-path lit up.

Having no radio, I could not ask permission to land; neither had I navigation lights on the Magister, a fact I discovered when it became dark and I looked in vain for switches. As I made my approach, a Blenheim twin-engined bomber suddenly shot past my nose, put his navigation lights on and proceeded to land. Thinking I could squeeze in behind him and land while the flares were still on I was met by a red Very light and had to veer away to find a second Blenheim coming in. I hurriedly circled to get in behind him and succeeded in this and in taxiing to the hangars before an infuriated officer in charge of night flying could catch me. However, apologies to the Station Commander and Squadron Commander put things right, and I was, at least, that much nearer Plymouth and my next period of watch-keeping.

To my great joy and satisfaction the last 'peacetime' form of promotion list, published January 1st, 1940, notified my promotion to Group Captain and I was posted back once again to Northolt to command. This was one of the London fighter stations with a Sector Operations Room and satellite aerodromes at Heston and Luton at times. I was kept busy, usually about sixteen hours every day, seven days a week, but it was a dramatic and stirring time that I would not have missed.

The Air Fighting Development Unit, as it was now called, was still at Northolt, commanded by an old friend, Wing Commander 'Tiny' Vasse, so-called, of course, because of his large size, and I was soon watching attack and defence methods with more up-to-date aircraft. An exercise 'Spitfires attacking Wellingtons' gave me my first chance to fly the Spit and the remark in my log-book on my first trip in one is 'enjoyable', which I am sure a great number of others have felt on their first occasion.

I also went on two or three occasions to Dengie Flats on the east coast to fire the guns in a Hurricane. The difference between my first air firing and this was staggering. The pop-pop-pop of the Lewis gun of the First War had been almost countable, but rapid fire of eight Browning guns firing simultaneously sounded like a quick tear of a piece of calico. I wondered if I would, as an old man of forty-three, ever have the chance, or the nerve, to fire them 'in anger'.

The next few months of the still 'phoney' war were taken up with training squadrons, arranging the aerodrome defences of Bofors gun positions, slit trenches, a defence Headquarters bunker, and fixing up a 'K' site—a dummy aerodrome a mile or so from Northolt where a flare-path could be put out to attract the night bombers away from the proper airfield—and it paid off a little.

Camouflage experts came to hide the hangars with paint and proposed their usual irregular strips of brown and green paint to break up the vertical and horizontal regularity of the buildings. With this I forcibly disagreed, pointing out that the aerodrome was surrounded by housing estates and buildings almost joining up with London—so all the enemy had to do to locate Northolt was to fly north-westerly from London until they came to an open area, and that would be it. What had to be done was to make it inconspicuous in its built-up surroundings.

After much argument they finally agreed, and the hangars were made into double rows of small houses by alternative pitch roofs being painted bright red with cream facings down to half-way of the sides, with black 'windows and doors' patches superimposed, and green gardens and black blob 'trees' on the lower parts of the walls and tarmac. The result was very satisfactory as we received no mass bombing by day, and only random bombing by night, yet during the fifteen months that followed 4,000 bombs (counting a stick of incendiaries as one bomb) were dropped within a two-mile radius of the hangars. We did have our casualties on the camp from both day and night bombing, but they were nowhere near as heavy as those at Biggin Hill, Kenley and Hornchurch.

So effective was our camouflage that even our own pilots, who knew the aerodrome well, failed to find it on occasions. To break-up the straight runways, we effected a 'stream' meandering from side to side, with a pond where the two runways intersected. Black blobs maintained an illusion of tree-lined banks until one got down to a few hundred feet, when the genuine runways were clear. The crowning glory of this scheme occurred when my clerk of works came into my office to say he had just seen two swans come in to alight on the 'water' and crash land!

During the period of aerodrome attacks a large formation of German bombers was plotted on the Operations Room table approaching on a straight course for Northolt and it is now known this was their intended target. Our squadrons at the time were all airborne intercepting an earlier raid east of London, so the Controller at No. 11 Group ordered two squadrons from North Weald, at the north end of Epping Forest, to patrol five miles south of Northolt with the intention of meeting the new threat. These two squadrons were led by Squadron Leader Grandy, who had been stationed in No. 24 Squadron at Northolt as a Flight Lieutenant only a few months previously. Both he and the Germans failed to find the aerodrome because of its effective camouflage and Brooklands was the unlucky recipient of the formation's bombs on the way out.

But that was later. During this preparation period I flew a Magister, Mentor, Master, Gladiator, Tutor, Spitfire, Vega Gull, Hurricane, Proctor, Lysander, Buffalo and Blenheim for a variety of reasons with an assortment of passengers.

11

Battle of Britain

In July came the evacuation from Dunkirk, and the Northolt squadrons took part in this extremely difficult operation. I flew down to Hawkinge, behind Folkestone, where they operated and refuelled, and we felt that the war was starting in earnest.

As it sometimes happened that our three squadrons were all engaged leaving the aerodrome empty and very vulnerable, I formed a Station Defence Flight. The personnel was to be any of us, in H.Q. or surplus from any squadron, who would seize any serviceable aircraft available to go up to endeavour to intercept any approaching enemy. I had been up on two or three occasions chasing departing raiders without any success, and to the amusement and delight of all airmen one day, the loud-speakers from our Sector Operations Room boomed out 'Station Defence Flight—Scramble!' I jumped into a Hurricane (which turned out to be the A.O.C.'s personal aircraft—Air Vice-Marshal Keith Park's). Vasse came up in a Gladiator and Campbell Orde in something also from No. 24 Squadron, and we were vectored on to a single Junkers 88 approaching from the south. Given his course and height, we soon got close but could not at first see anything but cloud. Eventually I spotted it through a gap in the cloud and my cry of 'Tally Ho!' in the Controller's earphones nearly deafened him. But the Ju88's crew also saw us, and immediately turned for home.

A long chase ensued, when Campbell Orde faded away followed by Vasse, who could not keep up with my Hurricane with its 'emergency boost' pulled. The Ju88 sought cloud cover as soon as I got anywhere near in range. I climbed to get the sun behind me, hoping he would not therefore see me when he next appeared, but I lost distance in doing so. This was repeated two or three times, until at last I fired three long bursts at far too great a range, in a desperate hope that something might strike home; but I suppose not, as the last I saw of him was getting back into the cloud bank. I only tell this very unimportant story as it was the first time I fired my guns at an enemy aircraft in World War II. The A.O.C. was most hurt when he found his aeroplane all oily after its long flat-out chase, but had to admit that it was a necessity.

Early in August No. 303 (Polish) Squadron formed at Northolt. They were then completely new to the Hurricanes, although all experienced in air-fighting in Poland. They had reached England by devious routes, escaping through France, Spain or North Africa to Gibraltar and thence by Royal Navy, or by other hazardous routes across Europe.

Unfamiliar with retracting undercarriages or flaps, we had a few cases of belly landings or over-shooting the aerodrome. Also, they could not understand enough English to be controlled from an Operations Room on the ground. Hating the Germans they simply wanted to get into the air as soon as possible and attack the first ones they saw. I could not declare them operational until they could understand English better, so they hated me! But they set to work with a will to learn the language for many hours each day as well as to get familiar with their aeroplanes, which they soon came to like very much, and consequently to fly well.

They had a British C.O.—Squadron Leader 'Boozy' Kellett—and two British Flight Commanders, Athol Forbes and Johnny Kent, who all got on splendidly with their new charges. On the last day of August a flight of six under Kellett was on a training flight when they sighted, to their surprise, six German aircraft immediately below them in the ideal position for an attack. This they proceeded to carry out and shot up every one, having caught them completely by surprise owing to intervening cloud. Wild and enthusiastic with excitement as they were, I had to lift the ban and make them 'operational' from then on. Immediately their results were amazing and claims for bombers shot down were so high that I told Wilkins, my Intelligence Officer, to vet them very carefully. Wilkins said that he already did so, but they did sound genuine and that they confirmed each other's claims.

I decided to watch them, having been out with several other squadrons previously and, sure enough, we were sent to a big enemy formation near the London docks. Two of the Poles were sent vertically above while the remainder waited behind —with me behind them. The two then dived vertically down into the bomber stream with guns blazing. The German pilots, seeing a collision was inevitable even should they survive the bullets, turned off left and right, so the formation was broken, their supporting fire sacrificed, and the Poles behind jumped in on to the scattered individuals and suddenly the air was full of burning aircraft, parachutes, and pieces of disintegrating wings. It was all so rapid that it was staggering. I pulled myself together, thinking I would have a chance to finish off some lame duck out on its own, but as soon as I started to close in on one—sure enough a diving Pole would cut in between and I had to pull away to avoid being hit myself!

I told Wilkins that what they claimed they did, indeed, get! They were a delightful light-hearted bunch, and loved an elementary type of joke—with their imperfect but rapidly improving English. For instance, one day at their dispersal area after a sortie, one of their number, Zumbak, had not returned, and they were worried about this and anxiously scanned the sky for his Hurricane. I said, 'Don't worry, Zumbak will "Kumbak",' which they thought was wonderful, and walked about repeating 'Zumbak will Kumbak'. Fortunately, my light-hearted prophecy was correct, and he did indeed come back, having had to land—damaged—at another aerodrome. He was one of the very small number of the original magnificent members who survived the war.

On another occasion a Sergeant Pilot—Frantisek—who was actually a Czech but flying with the Poles and had been remarkably successful in his many fights, was reporting a combat—

Shoreham, 1910. Piffard (*centre*) is standing next to the propeller; S.F.V. on the extreme right next to his brother and father

Maurice Farman 'Longhorn' with 70 h.p. Renault engine

Sopwith Triplane, a very light single-seater with a good rate of climb, as used at the South-East Area Flying Instructors' School in 1918

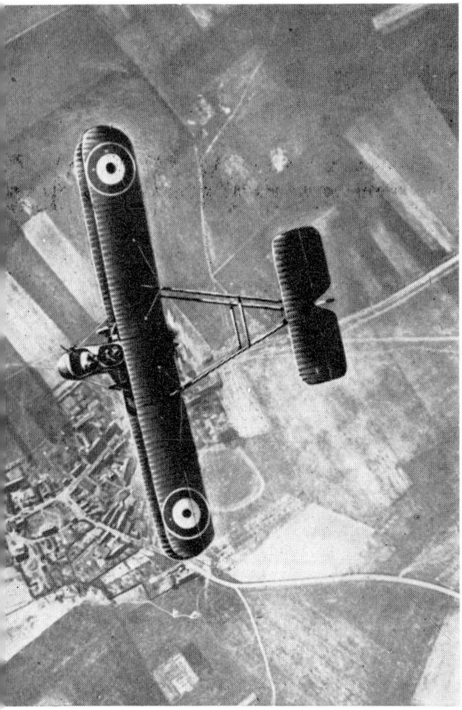

F.E. 2B in flight, a type used extensively for bombing and photographic reconnaissance during the First World War

This Christmas card, drawn by Roderic Hill, shows six Nieuports of No. 60 Squadron lined up in front of six Bessonaux hangers. The spinner (red in the original) on the near one identifies it as Albert Ball's

Sopwith Pup, a late production model

Bristol monoplane. This single-seater, lovely to fly, was years in advance of its time; although not used on the Western Front it served operationally in the minor theatres

Avros with the striped noses adopted as the marking of the Special Instructor's Flight and the South-East Area Flying Instructors' School

S.F.V. beside a Fokker DVII flown from France early in 1919

D.H.9A F2771 flying in Kurdistan, 1924—not the country for a forced landing!

Wapitis over Burma jungle. Singapore Flight, 1934

Rolls-Royce armoured cars of the R.A.F. in the Middle East between the wars armed, like aircraft of the period, with Vickers and Lewis machine guns

Dust of Shaibah as No. 84 Squadron takes off in formation in Vickers Vincents during the mid-thirties

King George VI in conversation with Air Vice-Marshal Keith Park, S.F.V., and a Polish pilot at R.A.F. Station Northolt in September 1940

King Edward VIII at Northolt, with Air Chief Marshal Sir Edward Ellington behind him and S.F.V. on right

The three services in Burma represented by Admiral Lord Louis Mountbatten, flanked by S.F.V. and General Sir William Slim

S.F.V. flies Air Marshal W. A. Coryton in a chequered Harvard to an airstrip in the forward area in Burma

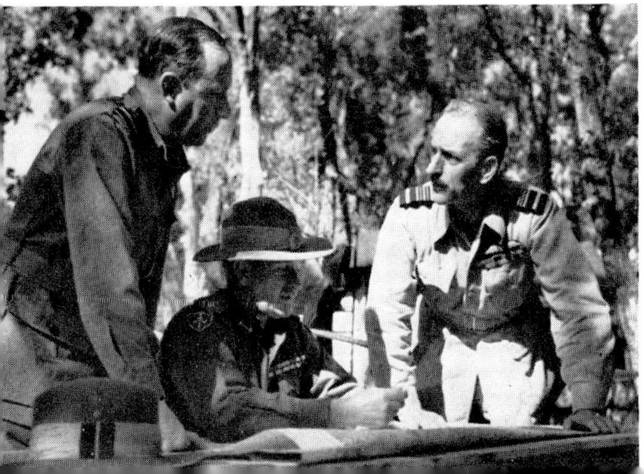

Jungle conference, Burma, early 1945. General Sir William Slim with Air Marshal Coryton (*right*) and S.F.V.

Six proud generals after the fall of Fort Dufferin, Mandalay.
Left to right: Maj Gen Nicholson, Maj Gen Wynford Rees, S.F.V., Lt Gen Slim, Lt Gen Stopford, Maj Gen Gracey

This Hurricane, LF 363, was specially built by Sydney Camm of Hawkers for S.F.V., No. 11 Group, 1948

'There was an Me110 on my tail but I took no notice of him.' I replied, 'You can't ignore a fighter on your tail—it's better to dodge and fight again another day.' 'But he could not fire at me,' he explained, adding, when I asked why, 'Because I was too close on the tail of a bomber.' It seemed he had killed the rear gunner of the bomber and was using it, calmly, as a 'shelter' from the escorting fighters by flying, very close, immediately behind it. . . . The fighters having eventually turned away, he shot down the luckless bomber in flames.

I was lucky one day when nibbling at a fighter-escorted raid to get mixed up with three Me109s and, after a fairly short time, I realised that the two followers were more keen on following their leader than splitting up and getting rid of me, so I considered I might be able to join them in line and shoot down each in turn. As I was almost getting into position to do just this, I saw No. 2 firing his guns—but at No. 1, which burst into flames and the pilot came out in his parachute; seconds later No. 3 was also jumping as I got his aircraft similarly in flames! Foolishly, I turned to watch the two going down to get a vague idea where they would land, and so missed the chance to get No. 2 as well. As a result I was credited with two Me109s. Whether No. 2 had been confused with the general twisting and mistook his No. 1 for me, or whether he merely hated No. 1's guts and took the opportunity to get rid of him over enemy territory, I shall never know. But it was pleasant to be helped by an opponent!

On the glorious September 15th, 1940, the peak day of the Battle of Britain, I was up both morning and afternoon. In the morning I wasted a lot of ammunition in taking pictures with my cine-camera gun—which worked when guns fired—as I saw a vast enemy formation of something over 100 bombers approaching, stretching over an area of about five miles. As they were silhouetted against the sky while I was still climbing, I thought it would make an impressive film, so I cocked my nose up and opened fire, swinging my nose from the front to the rear of the vast formation. I was well out of range for hitting anything with bullets. Later I did do some close-range firing and hoped for good pictures as well then. On landing, I sent the film to be developed, hoping for some really dramatic pictures, only to find that the focussing ring had been loose and unscrewed, so that the complete film was a blur. I was bitterly disappointed.

In the afternoon I was on the way to join one of the squadrons south-east of London when I saw a formation of eighteen Dorniers, escorted by twenty Me109s above, approaching unmolested from the south. Searching the sky in vain to see if any of our fighters had been assigned to them, I realised that I was in an ideal position for a frontal attack on the bombers and

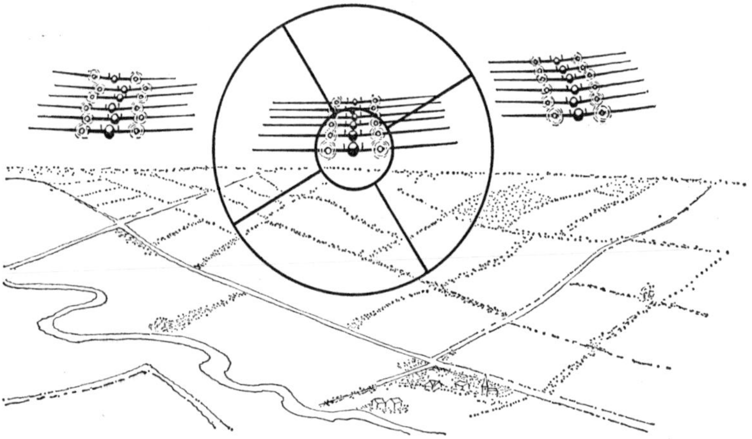

The 'too good' formation of Dorniers in my ring sight

that I could effect this before the escort could intercept—even if they had seen my single fighter below.

The bombers were in three lines of six craft in line astern and as I lined up on the centre line I could see six craft in the gunsight all merging into one target. Opening fire, I could see my De Wilde ammunition sparkling all over the leading bombers and I switched to my right as I started a half-roll and saw De Wilde on that side Dorniers as well. I passed very close below the formation. half-rolling downwards to get away from possible fighter attention, and as I dived down I saw bombs bursting in the corner of a field and into a wood, and appreciated that the formation had jettisoned their bombs.

When I eventually pulled out of my dive and started climbing again, I saw thirteen bombers only, turning back to the south, and no Me109s which had evidently departed to their proper target area. I saw no sign of the five missing ones as I was searching for the fighters, but *I* know I had shot down more bombers in a shorter time than ever before, though I could not claim them as I had seen none go down or crash—so now I commit the crime of 'shooting a line' which I have not been able to do before!

The branch of the Air Ministry responsible did say that four Dorniers had been collected within a ten-mile radius of that encounter, all shot down from the front with their pilots killed by .303 gunfire—unclaimed by anyone else. And German records show that KG76 lost five of their bombers operating over southern England. I escorted the thirteen out of the country and got one more of them dropping behind the remainder, further and further, though I couldn't do any more about him, having run out of ammunition. But German records show another of KG76's bombers crashing at Cap Gris Nez.*

Around this time, I was told a ferry pilot, who had just delivered a Hurricane, wanted to see me. In came Smith-Barry, my old C.O. of the First War, a Major when I was a Lieutenant, and Colonel when I was a Captain. Now rejoined as a Pilot Officer, he saluted and I saluted him equally and welcomed him joyously. The last time I had seen him was at a reunion party at Brooklands, with a longish grey beard, with his private Puss Moth aeroplane; but now he was back in R.A.F. uniform with a very thin stripe on his sleeve, while I had four fat ones on mine! We repaired to the mess for a celebratory glass of sherry before he went off to deliver something else to someone else. Shortly after this he was caught by low clouds while delivering a Blenheim IV and crashed into a hedge; but he came through,

* The German confirmation of these figures appeared many years afterwards—too late for an official claim.

to be made a Squadron Leader in charge of a satellite airfield. A great man.

Aircraft ferrying was becoming more and more a matter for the A.T.A.—Air Transport Auxiliary—with 'dug-out' pilots unfit for Active Service, and women pilots, who did a magnificent job delivering replacement aircraft to the squadrons from the depots. Casualties to aircraft would be reported at the end of the day; almost invariably, new replacements would arrive the very next day or the day after. All-night work by the ground crews would then have them ready, squadron letters on, guns and sights harmonised, ammunition in and waiting for the pilot who might have come down in his parachute in Kent, or even in the Channel, perhaps only 24 hours before.

At Northolt for a time I had two favourite nieces serving in the W.A.A.F. in the aircraft reporting role. On one occasion I had to have all the girls up for a 'fatherly' talk as some had not been behaving very well off duty. I walked up and down in front of the parade saying my bit, but was not a little disconcerted by meeting two pairs of twinkling eyes in the middle of the front rank! I could feel their thoughts, 'Poor old Uncle, he's really trying to do his piece!' With difficulty I kept a straight face and avoided giving them the usual avuncular kiss . . . which might not have been understood by the remainder!

One day, one of low cloud, a German bomber came out of the clouds at a few hundred feet and saw, I am sure to his surprise, hangars right in front of him. He let everything go as he went by. One bomb fell right in front of a taxiing Hurricane, killing an excellent Polish pilot who had shot down two enemy aircraft only the day before; another bomb went between two large hangars, killing a look-out on the roof. This man was standing with two others who were amazed to see him sail up into the air and fall back—dead—while they scarcely felt any blast at all. An ominous hole was made between the hangars with metal at the bottom so we cordoned off the area for 24 hours, waiting for the bang, but eventually dug down to find only the tail fin of the bomb that had long since done its worst. The enemy aircraft was, entirely due to the Observer Corps' accurate running commentary, caught and brought down before it reached the coast.

One night the loudspeaker, which broadcast reports from the look-out on the hangar roof, blared out: 'Rifle fire from the south-east corner of the aerodrome!' We in the Ops Room, two miles away, assumed it was another case of a Pole getting in through the wire and thought that a shot in his neighbourhood would deter him in future. However, the voice came in again with 'More shots from the south-east corner' and I began to wonder. When 'Machine-gun fire from the south-east corner' was reported I became thoroughly alarmed, thinking of parachute attacks, fifth columnists or something equally serious.

Hurriedly leaving in my car, with tin hat, automatic in holster, gas mask and all the paraphernalia suitable for the occasion, I found that the Orderly Officer had everything under control. Collecting and leading a party of armed airmen, he had separated two parties of Poles and Irish Guards (a company of whom were our aerodrome guards) who had got down to serious fighting at an 'Aerodrome Club' just outside. This had started with an argument between a Sergeant of each, over a girl dancing-partner. Supporters of each gathered outside the club and in a hectic five minutes or so rifles, a sub-machine gun, revolvers and knives had all come into use.

Going to the sick quarters, I found the M.O. and his orderlies in shirt-sleeves patching up both sides. Mercifully nobody was killed, and only one Irish Sergeant who was being sent off to hospital with a stab wound in his back that the doctor feared might have reached his liver or kidneys. He was lying on a stretcher, waiting for an ambulance, when I asked him how he felt.

He replied, 'Foine, sirr, it was a whonderful noight!'

So I said, 'Oh, you're all right,' and very fortunately further examination proved that he was.

I then kept the two units well away from each other. Speaking to the Irishmen on parade the following morning, I told them how every one of the Poles had reached this land through many different countries in Europe and North Africa, taking many risks in order to fight with us, not against us! I then had the interpreter tell the Poles how the Irish love a scrap, but that it doesn't mean anything and that it would be forgotten immediately. But my N.A.A.F.I. manager came to see me to say that the Poles had been in the canteen and had bought up all the razor-blades! So, thinking of these stuck into small pieces of wood, I had parties of armed airmen at all strategic points the following night. The club I had put out of bounds to all, but it was still watched as were all public houses within a small radius, and I was relieved when the next nights passed quietly.

The Guards Brigade in London thought it advisable to exchange the Irish for the Coldstream Guards, so everything quickly reverted to normal. I considered that the least said the soonest mended and did not report the incident to anyone, as I knew there would be Courts of Enquiry, with much difficulty and time-wasting, so all were told to keep quiet. To my intense relief only rumours trickled out and I did not have to account to anybody for my private war!

During the next few months I went out with No. 302 (Polish) Squadron, which arrived at Northolt in October to relieve No. 303 (Polish) Squadron, and was out with them one day in the middle of November on the way to join up with my other two squadrons, Nos. 229 and 615, over the Channel. When approaching Dungeness, Control informed me that there were four 109s ten miles south-west. Intended as a warning, I took it as information for action and as I turned in that direction I saw four contrails above, moving towards me. Thinking that I could get behind and below them, and climb up unseen to attack, I glanced behind in one of my frequent checks over my shoulder to see that there was no one behind me, and saw to my horror that I, too, had reached contrail height. A long white stream was giving away my position and spoiling my plan. Sure enough, the four contrails above stopped, indicating that the aircraft were diving. I searched the sky above, having dropped down myself until I was no longer advertising my position by the tell-tale white stream.

I circled round slowly, craning my neck. Suddenly I felt I'd been kicked in the middle of my back by a mule. Thoroughly winded, my immediate reactions were sound in that I did a half-roll and twisting dive before I had time to take the breath for which I found myself gasping. I pulled up with all my strength until I did see one of the four behind, but realising there were three more somewhere and I could not get a breath, I decided to 'live to fight another day', and dived vertically, on the twist from 26,000 feet to 4,000, taking about 8,000 feet of that to ease out of the dive.

When flying level again I anxiously scanned the sky around, took careful stock of the situation and set course for Northolt, thinking I could make it. I imagined that a shell from the 109 had hit my armour plate and knocked it off its fastenings with a bang against my seat, so winding me. Even when I felt a trickle of blood down my back, I thought a bruise was just oozing blood and that I would have a black and blue back to show for my foolishness.

Watching my instruments, I found the oil pressure steady and temperature correct, but when I looked at the hydraulic system indicators, between one's feet in the Hurricane, I saw a nasty steady ooze of thick oil which covered them, so I did not know if my flaps or undercarriage would function. My radio was dead, which was not surprising as that was immediately behind the armour plate and would obviously have been smashed first. I was, therefore, not able to tell Control what had happened, nor hear or answer their worried requests for news. On looking over the side of the cockpit, I saw more oil oozing over the wing close to the fuselage—so keeping a nervous eye on the pressure gauge, I flew on and passed by Kenley with tempting runways beneath.

Then, thinking that there was nothing but houses all the way from Kenley to Northolt, with not a chance of forced landing if the oil finished and my engine seized up, I turned back and landed. To my relief the undercarriage came down satisfactorily, though my flaps would not function, but by landing short I did not overshoot the runway. Somewhat gingerly, I got out and found a lot of damage aft, in the fuselage, tail and rudder, and gave thanks for the sturdiness of the good old Hurricane. With that damage it had withstood the dive away from the shooting, and I saw why it had taken so long to come out of the dive with what there was left of the elevators.

I was patched up at Kenley and returned by car to Northolt, thence to Uxbridge for an X-ray and on to Halton Hospital where some forty pieces of assorted shell, armour plate, aluminium seat, an armour-piercing .303 bullet and its copper sheath—separately—were removed from against my spine by the good Wing Commander Stanford Cade. Half an inch to the left and my spinal column would have been severed and I paralysed; half an inch to the right, bits would have reached lungs and heart. A gap in my log-book, therefore, of just over two months before the entry, 'With 601, 3 other squadrons and bombers to bomb Boulogne in Hurricane'. The last one I had borrowed from No. 302 (Polish) Squadron was a 'write off'.

I have been writing only of my very small share in the Battle—I only did this because I was shamed into the air by the young men who faced heavy odds day after day and week after week, with the nerve-shattering periods between 'Scrambles' on the ground at dispersal, waiting from early dawn to late dusk for that cursed telephone to order them to dash off again to their aircraft, possibly two or three times a day. I was in the position of being able to choose my targets and times with doing the usual office work in between running a station and also helping in the Operations Room and controlling a squadron in the air to get it into a favourable position, as quickly as possible, against an incoming raid.

The controllers were mostly 'dug-outs' who had previously served in the R.A.F., possibly in the First World War, and they, after a course on their control work, had regular watches, which they carried out with the greatest efficiency, getting to know their Squadron Leaders and Flight Commanders on the ground, and gaining their confidence so that co-operation between ground and air was efficient. There were differences, of course, such as when a formation leader wanted to attack an enemy formation to which other squadrons had been detailed by No. 11 Group H.Q. The controller then had to persuade him to leave what looked like a tempting target, in order to get him on further to tackle the one to which he was allotted.

On the whole the system worked remarkably well. The raid was first spotted by radar and reported as it climbed up over France. By the time it had set course, a fair estimate of numbers could be made. At this period No. 11 Group would give the raid a code number and detail a squadron or squadrons to attack. The sector concerned would order the aircraft up and give bearings, height and relevant information until they received the sighting 'Tally Ho' from the fighter leader, when the interception was left entirely in his hands.

Frequently fights took place over cloud and the pilots would have very little idea where they were; but by then, by calling up on their radio, they could be pinpointed by direction finders and given a course and distance to base. Their return from these sorties was always dramatic—perhaps one or more would fly over 'wagging their wings' up and down denoting a claim of an enemy (after the 'Victory Roll' had been forbidden as this manœuvre was dangerous with possibly damaged aircraft). Others would land with holes in wings and fuselage, sometimes a wounded pilot and a call for an ambulance. Then an excited talk, confirmation of successes, thanks for rescue, cursing for tardiness, while the Intelligence Officer tried to get a coherent report from each individual, and all the time airmen sweating away to refuel and rearm and perhaps patch up the superficial damage. Then there would be the aircraft late coming back, and those definitely overdue. Telephone calls would be made to other aerodromes seeking information and finally grim acceptance of the fact that there were casualties. The gaps at the mess table and at dispersal were terrible, but replacements came along and the losses couldn't be dwelt on, as young nerves could not stand it—so beer was drunk (but not nearly so much as many are fond of saying) and songs sung before bed and such an early morning rise again.

We had a night squadron at our Luton satellite entailing occasional visits and the Station Commander usually had about twelve to sixteen hours a day, seven days a week! The nights then were very often disturbed by bombing in and all round the aerodrome.

A fairly frequent visitor to Northolt was the Duke of Kent,

the R.A.F. member of the Royal Family, and occasionally the Duchess came with him, in order to fly off to some aerodrome on inspections. When he heard I was leaving the station he did me the great honour of ringing up to ask if he could come and say good-bye. He spent an hour or two—including a glass of sherry in the mess. Not long after, I was so very sorry to hear of his death, by being flown into a mountain in cloud over Scotland, when on his way to Iceland to visit the small R.A.F. detachment there.

Once or twice the Commander-in-Chief, 'Stuffy' Dowding, came to watch the night war in the Operations Room and we saw him frequently by day when he flew to visit his fighter stations; Northolt being the nearest both to Fighter Command and No. 11 Group Headquarters.

Another visitor on two or three occasions was Winston Churchill on his way from Chequers to London. He would visit the dispersals, chat with the pilots and invariably boost morale. On one occasion he told us, 'We have bombed Italy [this was before the news was published]. We bombed the railway at Naples' . . .pause . . .'and the railway station is right in the middle of the town.' Once he came with his wife and a few cabinet ministers to see new types of bomber which had been brought there for his inspection; he was so anxious that Mrs. Churchill should not miss anything of particular interest.

There was one glorious day when everything went right. H.M. the King came to visit us. On arrival, we had our own Home Guard company composed of our elderly Works and Buildings personnel, groundsmen, storemen, mess and other staff, mostly over-age civilians, drawn up as the first guard of honour. We were one of the few aerodromes with such a body, and we were very proud of their spirit and enthusiasm. They would, I am sure, have acquitted themselves well in the case of a parachute attack.

The three squadrons were all at dispersal, in flying kit, and the King spoke to many pilots and airmen. Hardly had we finished when the Civil Alert sounded, followed by orders for all three squadrons to scramble. I asked the King if he would like to follow the action in the Ops Room, then two miles away in two commandeered and combined shops. He was very keen to do so, so there we went, to the delight of the duty crew.

The King listened to the Controller instructing the Wing Leader and saw the counters moved on the table as our three squadrons approached the raiders. As they closed the Controller handed the earpiece to His Majesty advising that he should hear the 'Tally Ho' any moment. Very shortly the King's eyes sparkled with excitement as he said, 'He's given the Tally Ho!' He was very impressed as he heard the leader detail one squadron to occupy the enemy fighter escort, while a second squadron attacked the bombers, and the third was detailed to wait above to be brought in on the latter if possible, or help against the fighters if necessary.

He heard all the dramatic bits of talk which went on: 'Look out! Red 2—one on your tail!'—'I've got a flamer!'—'Watch those at 3 o'clock, Blue one', etc. The counters on the table, all mixed, of course, then turned and moved out of the country (from the neighbourhood of Southampton) and individuals started asking for a course to steer for base.

We returned to the aerodrome and saw them landing. The first one, from No. 229 Squadron, had a burst of bullet holes through his wing, with the metal all bent up. The pilot got out, not expecting to see the King, who was scheduled to have left some time earlier. He stammered a bit when asked how he had got on, and mercifully replied, 'Well, sir, I did manage to get a 109', and shook hands with his delighted King.

And so it went on—everyone returned with the exception of a pilot landed unhurt at Thorney Island with a damaged machine. Later I rang up Buckingham Palace to report that the Wing had shot down no less than fourteen of the enemy for no fatal casualties to themselves. The King was delighted, and called on Air Ministry for a full and detailed report.

12

Singapore surrender

The Station Commander at North Weald, Victor Beamish, was posted and the squadrons there, having had heavy casualties, the morale was low. Beamish was a particularly fine man and all the pilots had a very high opinion of him. I was sent to replace him in March 1941 and to endeavour to build up the squadrons to fighting fitness. No. 242 Squadron had had ill fortune for some time culminating with them being 'jumped' when over the Channel and five of them, including their C.O., were shot down into the sea.

They were billeted in a very fine mansion not far from the aerodrome and when I visited them and gave them a talk, I found them in a very disheartened condition. I asked No. 11 Group to send Whitney Straight from No. 601 Squadron to take over the Squadron . . . I had only very recently promoted him to take over a Flight there but, in spite of his short time as a Flight Lieutenant, I felt sure, with his wide experience of flying and 'managing', he would make a good C.O. in these difficult circumstances.

We gave the Squadron a short time-off for training up the replacements, and remarkably soon Whitney Straight had them back operationally, and anxious to get their own back. There were pilots from eight or nine countries in the Squadron.

I was only at North Weald for four months during which time I went on a few trips over the Channel with Nos. 56, 242, 3 and 71 squadrons. Returning from one of them I found my back getting very painful and could hardly sit in the office afterwards. I had to call in the M.O. who took me along to the local hospital where a chunk of metal and about half a pint of 'bad' liquid were removed. I was sent off to the old Palace Hotel, Torquay (then an R.A.F. convalescent home) for a month—but managed to get away after three weeks.

I then went to No. 11 Group H.Q. as 'Group Captain Ops' which job included 'Aerodrome Defence' entailing flying round the Group with Colonel 'Mossy' Preston the Defence Officer. On one trip, flying a Miles Whitney Straight cabin monoplane in glorious summer weather, I remarked that I couldn't think why people went into the Army when this was available. We had lunch, did our inspection, and started back to Northolt when clouds blew up. It got very dark, the rain started and finally thunder was banging away and it became very bumpy indeed just under the cloud. A flash of lightning apparently thirty yards right in front, with a simultaneous crash of thunder, made us sit up with a jerk, feeling that the end was mighty near. I shouted to him, 'I can't think why so many people come into the R.A.F. when the ground is just down there.' This, luckily, made him laugh and before long we battled through to Northolt and landed, still in deluging rain.

One item of interest came about in this time as Group Captain Ops which was the preparation of the operation to drop the artificial leg for Douglas Bader while a prisoner of war—'Operation Leg'. The Germans said that they would give safe passage to an aeroplane to do this, but A.V-M. Leigh Mallory rightly said that we were flying over their territory every day and didn't need any permission from them, and that we would do so when and where we wanted. I happily signed that interesting and somewhat historical operation order.

After only about a month in command, the Group Captain at Biggin Hill crash-landed with engine failure which put him in plaster with a broken back. I said to the A.O.C. that such an important station should not be without a Group Captain and suggested I go and hold the fort there, at least temporarily. So off I went to my third station ringing London. This only lasted a month, as I was promoted Air Commodore and went 'down the hole' at Fighter Command Headquarters as a 'Duty Air

Commodore' and worked a watch system with two others in the underground Operations Room, co-ordinating the Nos. 11, 12 and 10 Fighter Groups in their operations and being in charge of the Air Raid Warning organisation.

I used to point out to Air Marshal Sholto Douglas pretty frequently that a troglodyte existence wasn't my idea of a war, and could I not be found something above ground? Later, when on week-end leave at Eastbourne visiting my family, the C.-in-C. rang me up to say, 'Well, you've asked often enough to get out of the hole, now you've got it, and no mistake—You've been sent to Singapore.' This was a bit of a shock as this was January 1942 and it was already very obvious that Singapore was going to fall—and soon!

I left Mount Batten (Plymouth) in a Catalina flying boat, together with Air Marshal Sir Richard Peirse, nominated the new C.-in-C. Far East, Air Commodores Bill Williams and Jack Hunter, the former to be on Peirse's staff, and the latter to take over the bombers while I had the fighters. After a wide sweep over the Atlantic to avoid hostile aircraft, while we manned the guns in the blisters in turn, we arrived at Gibraltar after 10½ hours' flying. There we saw 'Simposh' Simpson who was in command, while we waited for dusk the following day so that we passed near Italy in the dark. When that time came, there was some very rough sea outside the harbour, so our pilot hoped to get airborne inside the harbour using every inch of available space. We charged through the harbour aiming for the narrow entrance where we were unfortunately still on the water. We struck the first wave with an almighty bang and hung on to everything—the second bang actually flung us into the air where we hung on precariously but we did manage to hold off, and gradually got safe flying speed. It was a shaky start to no less than 16 hours 40 minutes in the air through the night and storms, in considerable discomfort.

It so happened that before we reached the potential danger area near Italy we ran into a terrific thunderstorm, with deluging rain which, though uncomfortable and somewhat frightening, made us safe from enemy action. We came down to a few feet above the water in the blackness at virtually nil visibility, but saw, in the flashes of lightning, the white horses on great waves only a few feet below. I hoped our young pilot could keep us at such a low altitude without losing those few feet in a bump. The navigator anxiously watched his radar to avoid flying into the island of Pantellaria, but due to the interference caused by the big waves, he never saw the 'blips' indicating an island and we did not know which side of it we passed. We took it in turns to try and sleep on a stretcher but we all failed completely and were remarkably relieved to see the dawn bringing finer weather and a sight of the North African coast.

We flew past Tobruk and landed on the Nile at Cairo. Here I saw 'Mary' Coningham who asked me to stay there and take over the fighters in North Africa, pointing out that it would be impossible to be of any value in the 'sinking ship' of Singapore. It was very tempting. I also saw 'Rosy' Rosier who had been one of my Squadron Commanders at Northolt and was now doing a grand job as a Wing Commander in the desert.

After two very welcome nights' rest we left—in great comfort this time—in the B.O.A.C. Empire flying boat *Corinthian*, passing over the old familiar route to the lake at Tiberias where we joined several members of General Laverack's Australian Divisional H.Q. Staff. We flew on to the lake at Habbaniyah where we saw more of my old friends, John D'Albiac, in command there, Eric Digby Johnson and Tom Harry England, but only while we refuelled before continuing to Basra, where we spent the night in an air-conditioned hotel, very different from my earlier days there. The next day on again over very familiar country, the Persian Gulf—to Bahrain, Dubai, and so to Karachi.

The following day we crossed India via Allahabad and Gwalior to Calcutta, and the next day to Akyab and Rangoon where I was pleased to see Stevenson and Manning, who seemed to be doing quite well, though I found out later that this was due to a few aircraft they had kept en route for Singapore for where they were intended and very urgently required! We spent the night in the aircraft at Port Blair in the Andaman Islands and were very hot and sticky and extremely uncomfortable. Early in the morning we left for Sibolga on the west coast of Sumatra, and finally to Batavia in Java. We were met there by air raid sirens as we had also been at Rangoon.

Here Jack Hunter and I left the rest of the party and carried on in another Empire flying boat up to Singapore. Our pilot—feeling very unarmed and conspicuous—flew all up the swampy jungle coastal plain of Sumatra at such a low altitude that we were actually in the steam seen to be rising from the swamp—we soon felt like a steamy swamp ourselves. Much relieved we at last arrived at Singapore, again to the wail of air raid sirens.

Feeling rather like relieving heroes come to save the situation, I rang up A.V-M. Pulford, the A.O.C. there, to let him know we had arrived, to be flattened by the news that he didn't even know we were coming. However, on going to Flagstaff House where he lived—also General Percival—it was decided to send Hunter away at once to Sumatra to try to organise the few bombers remaining, while I should stay to endeavour to get the few fighters reorganised and functioning.

Every day the Japs came over in majestic 'display formations' of twenty-seven, escorted by fighters and above the range of the 3-inch anti-aircraft guns—the only ones. They carried out pattern bombing of the aerodromes and docks. There was insufficient warning to get the few worn-out fighters into the air from the badly damaged aerodromes to achieve interception and so these formations usually sailed out unmolested.

It was exasperating; one could only stand and stare. The bombing often continued by night. Seletar aerodrome was soon mostly out of commission and Kallang completely so. The latter, the civilian airport, was on land reclaimed from the sea, with a crust only a few feet thick of mud on bamboo, which took the weight of aircraft satisfactorily, but when a bomb hit it there was left a large hole that could not be filled by pouring in soil or gravel, but had to have more bamboo 'weaved' into the bottom layer, and then filled over that. This, of course, took much too much time to be practical, and it had to be abandoned.

It was painfully obvious that the enemy would very soon be

in the island as some of the raw, untrained Australian troops were faring badly in Malaya; instead of putting up any resistance, numbers were arriving in twos and threes, many having thrown away their arms being completely demoralised.

The Argyll and Sutherland Highlanders, at the end of January 1942, were the last to leave the mainland and cross the causeway into the island of Singapore, proudly marching in threes with pipes playing. The Japanese were not far behind and the island was soon invested.

The following day it was decided that I should go to Sumatra with what was left of the fighters and try to carry on the war from there . . . somehow! With the usual strange contrasts that seemed to occur so frequently in this particular campaign, I had a very nice tea at Flagstaff House, sitting in a deck-chair in the garden, eating thin bread and butter with Chivers' strawberry jam with fine china—to the sound of booming guns.

I found out all I could from Intelligence of what I might expect in Sumatra, and fixed up for what equipment could be put into ships to follow us to Palembang, where apparently there were two landing-strips, P1 and P2. Next day I was taken in a Hudson twin-engined communication aircraft to P1, after a somewhat hair-raising take-off, swinging one way then another to dodge bomb-craters.

Accompanying me was Wing Commander Barclay who was to be my Senior Air Staff Officer of a newly formed No. 226 Fighter Group, Squadron Leader Roberts to arrange radar cover and Major Overell to fix up communications generally, also a N.A.A.F.I. representative to see to provisioning everyone that we hoped would soon be joining us by sea. The following day about forty Hurricanes arrived, being the remains of several squadrons, mostly from Nos. 232 and 258 Squadrons and a tremendous task started to get these operational.

We had only a handful of airmen to start with—with no accommodation, cooking facilities, dispersal huts or slit trenches; not even any water on the spot. The defences were about two platoons of Dutch territorial troops with four Bofors guns; we lacked heavy anti-aircraft guns, tool-kits and equipment such as trestles, oxygen for high flying and glycol

H

for engine cooling. Even transport was lacking, making the situation almost hopeless. However, the oil installations at Palembang fortunately refined the oil to the correct octane figure for our engines, and we were able to get petrol and oil there without charge, as it was clear that the Japanese would very shortly overrun the place.

I found a very helpful Dutch senior resident and we went round commandeering everything we needed, cars, schools and buildings for sleeping-quarters, blankets and even clothes, and quite quickly things became more habitable, though pilots and airmen were frequently hungry.

The Dutch had a small Operations Room in Palembang with a single—and bad—telephone line to the aerodrome at P1. There were no lines from there to dispersal points, so signals from the Duty Pilot to the stand-by pilots had to be arranged. The radio to the aircraft was most unsatisfactory as the only transmitter was some distance away in the Navy building, and orders to pilots had to be telephoned there and re-transmitted by someone else—usually a Dutchman who had never done this before. The receiver, a small private one in the Operations Room, was much affected by the daily heavy electrical storms. Within a week we managed to get our own transmitter and receiver in the Ops Room, with much better results.

13

Sumatran struggle

The Japanese very soon found out that we were there, and with the conditions already described and with very raw and inexperienced pilots who had joined us from Java—practically straight from Operational Training Units—it is not surprising that we suffered casualties that were inevitable and unavoidable. There were no battery-charging facilities, ammunition supplies were very low, and a lack of shelter from the heavy rainstorms which really deluged us daily. Poor No. 226 Group had a very bad start.

Every day I went to the aerodrome to try to 'encourage' and on two days in succession I had to watch helpless while three Hurricanes were shot down by Zeros. Owing to insufficient warning and the pathetically bad communications I watched these gallant lads trying to take off in time to attack, only to be shot down before they had climbed to combat height.

The Zeros flying from bases about 350 miles distant would jettison their long-range auxiliary petrol tanks and keep overhead for thirty-five minutes, machine gunning our strip, ignoring the feeble efforts of the Bofors guns. On the second day of their attacks they destroyed six Blenheim bombers and three Hurricanes, and damaged eleven more Hurricanes, a Buffalo and a Hudson twin-engined transport. A luckless Blenheim coming in to land was also shot down alongside the strip. The aerodrome presented a very sorry spectacle when the raid was over, with burning and damaged aircraft all round, and it did present a difficult problem to maintain any sort of morale, but while more slit trenches were dug (and this needed no encouragement!) we got the wrecks moved off the actual strip to avoid the miserable view.

When the enemy duly appeared again the day after we had filled in the bomb craters and were functioning, much the same thing happened all over again, though not quite to the same devastating extent. I was with a group of officers trying to move a Hudson which had had both tyres punctured by splinters while being refuelled from a tanker. The tanker was ablaze and we were endeavouring to save the aeroplane. We succeeded in this, but a Blenheim fully 500 yards away was also on fire.

I had driven past the Blenheim in my car shortly before, and having noticed it was bombed up, ordered everyone away. The bombs exploded with a tremendous roar and an airman standing beside me gave a cry of pain, for a bomb splinter had come that great distance and pierced his wrist, and was protruding on both sides. A curious reaction from this episode acted in our favour. The local natives working for us—filling bomb-craters, dragging wrecked aircraft away and so on—were so impressed by the magnitude of the blast compared with the smaller Japanese anti-personnel and incendiary bombs that they worked much harder, considering that we were doing much more damage to the Jap than he was to us!

After one more—not so serious—raid when there were no casualties, we had a very welcome draft arrive from England with the ground personnel of Hurricane squadrons and their tool-kits and other equipment. This fresh blood stiffened morale generally as the airmen would work on the aircraft up to the last minute, nip into slit trenches during the raid and carry on immediately after instead of running off into the jungle for an hour or more, as did some of the bomb-shocked ex-Singapore men.

Wing Commander Maguire arrived with this draft and flew up from Java with seven Hurricanes and was made Wing Commander Flying; he proved to be a first-class officer. On Friday 13th we were again attacked but I had previously convinced the superstitious that it was my lucky day. We had our Radio Telephony working ground to air and had earlier warning from one embryo Observer Corps member by telephone from further north. With new blood and aircraft we intercepted a raid, shooting down two bombers and three Zero fighters. With the exception of a solitary bomber we repelled the attack for the loss of a Hurricane and one pilot.

We felt we had turned the corner and had got the Japs' measure, and a great difference was immediately apparent in the morale of pilots and ground crew alike. For some evenings I had given talks to the pilots on tactics and it really seemed to be having effect. During this time we had not just been sitting on the ground waiting to be attacked, we had carried out fighter sweeps over the sea and Banka Island, escorting ships going to and from Singapore to protect them from enemy aircraft.

On February 14th for some reason I was not out at the aerodrome but in our little Operations Room some distance away. Our Observer stationed about 100 miles north reported a very large force of raiders approaching, with larger than usual aeroplanes, and flying very low. Accordingly I warned the aerodrome Defence Officer that it looked like a parachute attack, and ordered him to issue rifles and ammunition to all immediately. Shortly afterwards the sirens sounded, the guns fired and the gun liaison officer looked up from his 'phone to the guns, with a white face, reporting that 'hundreds of parachutes' were coming down all round.

Unfortunately all the Hurricanes were away escorting our bombers attacking a fleet of Japanese vessels approaching 'our' river. This was on the order from Java and against my wishes, as we should not have been left entirely unprotected. Within five minutes our only telephone line to the aerodrome was cut and we were completely in the dark as to what was going on.

As Senior Officer in the country I tried desperately to evolve some brilliant defence scheme. I could only think of the comparatively small number at the P1 aerodrome under Wing Commander Maguire, and that we must reach them. I got hold of Colonel Vogelensang commanding the small Dutch force, and got him to agree to send what men he would with rations and ammunition. We then embarked as a convoy of three lorries full of troops with rifles, a van with the food and ammunition, and my commandeered touring car. I ordered that if we were fired on from the jungle, everyone should blaze away in that direction, and we would be certain to get through. We were only about four miles short when we found the road blocked by a petrol tanker and lorry whose drivers had been killed, and rifle-fire came from the jungle on one side.

The only one hit was the R.A.F. van driver who swerved across the road and got ditched. The Dutch lorry-loads fired not a shot, and their drivers turned round and drove off leaving us to bring the two from the van, one hit in the arm, and return with ignominy after the supposed escort, leaving the supplies to the Japs. I was disgusted and ashamed, and drove out on the other road to P2 aerodrome where Hunter had the bombers. To my intense relief I found that road open. I put them in the picture, warning them to be armed against a similar attack there and returned to Palembang.

Seeing the Dutch Colonel again, I told him what I thought of him and his men. He said they could do nothing in the dark in the jungle, with which I could not but agree but insisted that we should try again in the morning and arranged a rendezvous. I went to bed about midnight in my hotel—a room with a balcony on the first floor. The manager and all the staff had flown and an eerie quiet surrounded the place. I fell asleep wondering whether a Japanese face was going to appear over the balcony at any minute.

At 5.30 hrs I went to the rendezvous to find the Colonel and all his gallant soldiers had flown. I got my few staff officers together and we decided that we should all go to P2 aerodrome where we would at least be altogether, so with heavy hearts we took all we could and left our men behind out at the aerodrome. We could not do otherwise.

Meanwhile enemy ships had arrived off the mouth of the River Mosei on which Palembang stands and an invasion force was starting up river in barges. Hunter flew off to Java to inform the C.-in-C. of the state of affairs in Sumatra, urging me to go with him, as it was painfully obvious that nothing could be done to save the situation. However, I refused, as it would have meant leaving all the others leaderless and deserted.

I went to see the big oil refinery and suggested that they turned the oil into the river and then the petrol on top of that and then set it alight, so that it would travel downstream and engulf the invasion barges coming up. Palembang was more than 50 miles from the coast and should this have come off successfully, the invaders that escaped the fire would have been stranded in swamp without food or supplies of any sort. However, this was said to be difficult and probably not even possible, so the attempt was not made; instead the tanks were set alight, and horrifying columns of black smoke went up in the air to well over 10,000 feet.

The bombers made a last sortie over the invasion fleet and caused considerable damage before flying down to Java, and the Hurricanes made several extremely successful attacks on the barges, undoubtedly causing many casualties. Only one pilot was wounded, being hit in the leg, but he succeeded in bringing his Hurricane back safely.

To get from Palembang to P2 aerodrome we had to cross the Mosei which was about a quarter of a mile wide. There was only one ferry and this could only take four vehicles at a time; as we had ambulances, anti-aircraft guns and many lorries and cars it was a very slow business, especially as the local crews had to be 'persuaded' to continue working. In addition, many civilians were also trying to get across, many with their own private cars.

The area got completely congested with abandoned vehicles An ambulance arrived late with a stretcher case, a sick airman. It was obvious that the ambulance could never get aboard as we were nearing the last of the troops, and no one had the heart to tell the casualty that we would have to desert him. They asked me to tell him this which, hating every second, I proceeded to do, saying no doubt the Japs would look after him quite well, and so on. He begged me to get the ambulance over the river, but I had to tell him that it was physically impossible to do so, and wished him the best of luck. However, he preferred to die among friends, so temperature of 104 or no, he got out, wrapped a blanket round his pyjamas, and boarded the ferry! I was very pleased to hear later that he got to medical attention at P2 and was passed on to the coast.

At long last I withdrew the airmen posted to watch for the approaching Japanese, who must have been very near then, and joined them in the last ferry to cross, with a full load of all that could squeeze aboard. We left a burning town with the oil refinery blaze capping everything. Among the abandoned vehicles which were jammed and impossible to get aboard, was a lorry with all my kit excepting a small suitcase of changes of underclothes, washing and shaving gear, so I reluctantly presented someone unknown with that—I hope it was a local and not a Jap. We tried to smash the engines of the vehicles left so that they would not be of use to the invaders.

On the day of the parachute attack a number of pilots bringing up much-needed reinforcements, had unfortunately been caught with empty petrol tanks just as they arrived and four were lost. One of them later gave me this account. 'Nine of us, led by Flt. Lt. Hutchinson, were ordered to leave Batavia for Palembang at 06.00 hrs on Saturday, February 14th. Unfortunately on our way to the aerodrome we had truck trouble and were unable to take off at schedule and left at rather a dangerous time (07.00 hrs), expecting the Japs, if over, to attack at 09.00-09.30 hrs each morning. Nearing Palembang we encountered low cloud, but came out together over the town and making for our base, P1. Between the town and aerodrome we ran into aircraft everywhere. I noticed a formation of what appeared to be our Hudsons 2,000 feet above, but which turned out to be Jap paratroop transports with Zero fighters as escort. We scattered immediately as we only had approximately 10–15 gallons of petrol left and our base was surrounded by paratroopers; four of our Hurricanes made for P2 about 40 miles away. I was flying a few feet above the high jungle when two Zeros attacked—the first got me in the left leg and the second in the right leg and arm and ended by shooting the tailplane of my aircraft off. I went into the jungle and hit very hard. Luckily mud and two feet of water took the engine and I lost one wing coming through the trees and ended upside down.

'All I noticed of the aircraft was one wing, the cockpit and a bit of fuselage. I pulled my harness pin and just fell out into the water and slush. I found I was in very dense jungle both high and low, and after a rest set out on a compass course. [He does not mention that during the 'rest' he had to cut out his compass from an upside-down aircraft in swamp.]

'After travelling for an hour and making very little progress, I had to give up as the jungle then was practically impassable. I then returned to my machine and gathered my dinghy and case to use as a battering-ram. This was most useful in flattening the seven-foot scrub and I started on another course. I was unable to call for help or fire my revolver as I knew Jap paratroops were somewhere in the vicinity. After travelling four hours and again making very little progress, perhaps two miles, I heard a cock crowing and immediately set my compass by it. I finally reached a small area of water deep enough to inflate my dinghy, mainly to get a rest free from ants, bugs and millions of mosquitoes. This led me to a large river which I paddled across reaching two native huts. The natives housed themselves as soon as they saw me, but came out willingly when told I was English. They rowed me down the river to a native village. The natives were exceptionally good, supplying me with beer and cigarettes. After a wait of about two hours, a Dutch truck arrived and took me in to Palembang, 12 miles away, and then to hospital.

'The next morning, Sunday, February 15th, more paratroops were dropped and we evacuated at 11.00 hrs; the wounded spent three days on the roads before arriving in Batavia. Our medical officers were marvellous, sleeping very little during those three days and doing everything possible for us. I spent four days in the Princess Juliana Hospital at Batavia and from there shipped home to Australia via Colombo. Here I hope to be able to join the old squadron again and serve under Squadron Leader Brooker, the finest C.O. and leader one could wish for.'

While most of us were making our way from Palembang to P2, those cut off at P1 were having a very bad time. The aerodrome defence personnel did well—they went out to meet the enemy parachutists before they could concentrate and killed many of them. They found several wriggling at the ends of their lines with their parachutes caught up in trees. These they left still hanging—but no longer wriggling. Sheer numbers, however, beat them and they had to concentrate on the strip, soon finding that they were cut off both by telephone and road.

After an hour or two, seeing khaki-clad figures approaching confidently, Wing Commander Maguire walked to meet what he presumed to be Dutch troops, only to find that they were Japanese! A parley followed, the Japs telling the Wing Commander to surrender and the Wing Commander telling the Japs that *they* must do so, as he had a large force over the brow of the hill and more were on their way from Palembang. Reaching an impasse, Maguire said he would go and consult with his senior officer and return to let them know the answer. He then went back over the brow of the hill where he told the small party of twenty airmen to turn their lorry round and give up any idea of trying to get through to Palembang, and to go in the opposite direction.

Against the advice of his senior N.C.O.s, he then went back to tell the Japs that they had better look out for themselves as they would soon be surrounded and killed. He then walked back to the lorry feeling rifles aimed at his back, and resisted, with great difficulty, the urge to run.

As the party had by then set fire to the few remaining aeroplanes and fuel store, they drove off in the lorry, eventually reaching the west coast after several days, nursing one airman with a broken arm caused by falling off the lorry. By good fortune they found a wireless station on the coast and were able to get a message to Java, whence a Royal Navy destroyer was dispatched to collect them. Maguire, unfortunately, was captured later in Java.

After reaching P2 we decided to get everyone out of this undefended country and every vehicle that we could muster was collected for the 200 miles to the port at Oosthaven. One officer fortunately found and commandeered a train with a crew. While our sick and wounded and as many airmen and gunners as possible were got aboard, the local crew were kept on duty by 'revolver coercion' and all made the journey that night.

The road party, after again burning unserviceable aircraft and fuel stocks, saw the last of the serviceable aircraft on their way to Java and left at dusk for the long trek in overcrowded vehicles. The road wasn't too bad and a reasonable speed was kept up through jungle practically all of the way. At night monkeys, disturbed by the long succession of lights, screamed at us as we passed. One carload of ten thought they would take a brief rest out of their vehicle and lay down beside the road, but were rudely disturbed by the savage roar of a tiger . . . they decided they were not as tired as they thought.

There were many chaungs on the way with small bridges over a very sudden and steep-sided drop to a stream. To prevent a rapid Japanese pursuit we had those blown up after the last vehicle had gone by, by our engineers using 500 lb aircraft bombs.

We arrived at the port early in the morning after an all-night drive. Having driven my commandeered touring car all the way I shut my eyes while still at the wheel and slept solidly for an hour. A number of us went into the local hotel hoping for breakfast, but found it deserted with the exception of one small and very friendly monkey who badly wanted a fuss made of it. We searched the larders and found only a dozen or more loaves, so a bread and water breakfast it had to be.

Then I saw to my dismay that the townspeople were already adopting a scorched earth policy and shops, warehouses and oil containers were going up in smoke and flames. I rushed off to the senior Dutch representative to get him to stop this idiotic panic destruction, but he was feeble in the extreme and, I suspected, even a fifth columnist, and nothing was done.

The most serious part of it was the way many Dutch, who were understandably fleeing the country, had taken their cars to the dockside and there slashed their tyres and hammered the engines and radiators so that they formed a barrier between our road and the quayside. There were, fortunately, still four or five ships that the embarkation staff were able to get us all on to and a certain amount of stores and guns, but we had to leave a complete lorry load of valuable engine spares and a complete engine which could not be dragged past the mass of immovable cars—to which we finally added ours similarly immobilised.

I left in the last ship to leave, the *Silver Larch*, about 03.00 hrs after several nights with practically no sleep, much travelling and great worries. The wonderful Scottish skipper said, 'You look as though you want some sleep—here's my cabin and there's a bottle of whisky, make yourself at home.' I had a small nip, put my head on his pillow and knew no more for four hours, when I gave over the bunk to a Brigadier who, in a similar condition, was queuing up for the bunk!

Going up on to the bridge I found the gunners had succeeded in getting four Bofors guns aboard, two in the fore well-deck and two aft, facing port and starboard in each position. The Captain then told me that he had a load of 300 tons of liquid mustard gas below near the bows! I did not pass on this alarming information to the others, but watched anxiously for the expected enemy bombers. Sure enough, two appeared but luckily ignored us, evidently having some other target in mind. I think the Bofors gunners were disappointed that they could not give the surprise they had planned.

As we were about to sail along the north coast of Java in broad daylight, I proposed to the Captain that, in view of the mustard gas, it would be wise to disembark the personnel at Merac on the western tip of the island. The *Silver Larch* went on with her load of liquid mustard gas, the Bofors guns and several tanks under cover of darkness that night. The port of Batavia, Tanjong Prioc, then refused to allow such a dangerous cargo to enter, so back they went out to sea again where they dumped the mustard gas drums in deep water and returned to off-load tanks, guns and spares.

The Dutch produced a few trains which we filled and slowly made our way to Batavia arriving in the early night. It was embarrassing that at the various stations at which we stopped, we were cheered and welcomed by the locals as reinforcements coming in. About midnight we found some empty Dutch barracks where the men could lie on the floor, there being no beds, and some rations of sorts. We were unexpected and no arrangements had been made.

I was taken with another officer by a Dutchman to their Broadcasting House, where I slept on a couch in a studio, quite well until 06.00 hrs, when I had to move to allow a pianist to perform. The next night I spent uncomfortably in a dirty hotel before going to H.Q. at Bandoeng, to see Sir Richard Peirse again to find out his appreciation of the situation and what airfields I had.

As a climax to the Sumatra story, after a few days a party under Squadron Leader Ramsay Rae took a small ship back to Oosthaven and, from the deserted port, managed to extract quite a useful amount of equipment, including the lorry-load of engine spares, and bring it back in triumph to Batavia. This was a particularly good show as they were not to know whether the Japs had arrived first. They concluded, rightly, that the blowing of the bridges had held up their advance from Palembang.

14

Java in jeopardy

Under peacetime conditions the road up to Bandoeng must be one of the most beautiful motor trips in the world. It climbs up out of the heat and damp of Batavia with good surface for about 3,000 feet, with glorious scenery in fertile well-kept countryside, with contented-looking natives. We had a marvellous lunch en route in the most beautiful of hotels, cool and dry, with magnificent views, a golf course, tennis courts and a swimming pool.

In Bandoeng we stayed the night in the Savoy-Hohnann Hotel where Sir Richard Peirse told me he had, the previous night, had the best dinner he had ever eaten in any hotel in the world. I found it was in every respect up to this standard, marvellous food and orchestra, unlimited staff, cool comfortable bedrooms with private bathrooms and every convenience. Charming demoiselles in beautiful evening frocks combined to make it hard to believe that we had been running away in acute discomfort for several days and nights . . . and that the enemy was advancing towards us as fast as he could manage.

I returned to Batavia the following day and moved into the Hotel des Indes which was very much the same style as the Savoy-Hohnann. Here I stayed for a fortnight in luxury, living a most extraordinary existence, in that during the mornings I was frequently shot-up and bombed out at one of the aerodromes—in fact one day I had one of the closest shaves of my life—to be followed immediately after—having brushed the dust of the slit trenches from my clothes—by a luxurious lunch with orchestra playing in the company of exquisitely dressed ladies and their escorts. The hotel and its residents completely ignored the air-raid sirens—I wondered whether they had an arrangement with the Japanese not to bomb the town. It never was bombed; all the attacks were confined to the port at Tanjong Prioc or the airfields Tjisaock, Tjileungsip and one near Buitenzorg.

Our main fighter airfield was at Tjililitong around which we dispersed our Hurricanes and Bofors guns and dug slit trenches. We took over a house and made a small Operations Room which we had functioning in little over a week, with direct radio contact with the aircraft and telephone links with a number of observer posts, on direct lines arranged by the Dutch. H.M.S. *Exeter* also became a very vital link in our chain, usually from about 100 miles north, giving us early warning of formations heading in our direction.

In this favourable position we were able to bring off several successful interceptions of raids and also obtain something like Battle of Britain figures for enemy shot down in relation to our smaller casualties. The building was surrounded by an unclimbable spiked bamboo fence and the Dutch works people did a first-class job in a remarkably short time. In addition, a squad of some twenty Dutch girls were trained in a week to become our plotters and filterers. A very attractive collection, they were most keen to wear uniform. They paraded before me in their creations for selection: drill blouses with short skirts, long trousers or mini shorts! I chose the trousers! On one item they all agreed—could they wear the R.A.F. fore and aft cap? I said they certainly could if they made them as we had none in our stores! However, they never had the chance as the Operations Room very soon had to be broken up and communications wrecked as the enemy once more approached.

During the last week or two we managed to reorganise the squadrons into two good units and started evacuating air and ground crew that could not be employed due to lack of aircraft, so that they could escape to carry on the war elsewhere.

One morning at Tjililitong, having just seen our Hurricanes off to a high raid over the port, I stood watching the distant anti-aircraft bursts and wondering if our fighters would attain height in time to intercept, when I chanced to look to my left and saw a gaggle of Zero fighters coming in at about a hundred feet. I shouted to those around to take cover and stooped to pick up my helmet at my feet; because of this brief delay I was the last to reach the slit trenches about ten yards away. The leading Jap saw us running and as I was diving for a trench I saw his guns firing. I landed full length on top of a Sergeant as an exploding .5 bullet hit the side of the trench about a foot above.

The pilot, evidently realising he was attacking across these small trenches, did a circuit and came in again to fire along the length of them. Again three or four strikes came about a foot below the rim at the end of the trench, but we were almost underground by then and were only spattered with earth. We were then able to watch the rest of the attack and were glad that the Hurricanes were away. One Hurricane did return before the Zeros left and he chased them out of the area. When he came back again he was fired at, and fortunately missed, by our own A.A. guns. One gunner was killed in the Bofors position near our trenches.

After seeing our squadrons back and hearing their reports, I returned to my hotel for a luxury lunch and soft music—it seemed so fantastically silly!

In the latter half of February, Air Vice-Marshal Maltby, who by then was A.O.C. West Group, known as 'Brit Air', called a conference at which the order of evacuation of the country was decided, as it was obvious all could not get away in the time with the ships available. Surplus pilots of operational squadrons were to be got away after fighting to the last possible moment, followed by repair depots, etc., with my No. 226 Group H.Q. well down the list. The bombers could fly out to Australia, but the fighters with their limited endurance had to fight to the last and then burn their aircraft.

We appreciated that our chances of being on an officially designated ship were practically nil, but it seemed unnecessary to be a prisoner if we could possibly avoid it, so I fixed up with about a dozen of us, including an M.O., to try to escape to

Australia in Flight Lieutenant Morton-Brown's yacht which was on the south coast. Captain Heath, R.N., and a naval Lieutenant were of the party and could produce the necessary instruments and be responsible for navigation. My S.A.S.O., Wing Commander Barclay, and others, were detailed to arrange for rations, water, fuel, medical and other supplies and transport to the south of the island. The yacht had an auxiliary motor which we intended to use all one night, to be as far out to sea as possible by daylight.

After a few days of planning, we began quite to look forward to our escape. It did not, however, take place as A.V-M. Maltby came to see us and was so favourably impressed with the fighters, Ops Room and general organisation, that he told us that although official evacuation was finished, there seemed to be no object in my H.Q. and staff staying to become prisoners as there were one or two ships left at Tjilatjap on the south coast so we were told to get moving.

Accordingly I went to see my gallant 'Fighter Boys' to say good-bye to them, and wrote letters to those I was unable to visit, to say how I was seemingly deserting them at their very worst hour, and exhorting them to fight to the last moment. Feeling simply dreadful, I left them to it, and they did, in fact, do a magnificent job flying many sorties each and every day, causing very heavy casualties to the crowded invasion barges, until, with heavy hearts, they finally burned their aeroplanes and 'went into the bag'. One had to be practical, of course, and say there was no virtue in remaining to become a prisoner if one could manage to get away and 'live to fight another day' and fortunately I was able to do just this and to get my own back on the Jap in Burma. After making out my final report on the evacuation from Sumatra and what had happened since, I went with a few carloads to H.Q. at Bandoeng to say good-bye and hand in the report. . . . I doubt if it ever reached the Air Ministry.

We planned to stay the night at H.Q., but were warned that if we did not get along immediately there would be no ships left at Tjilatjap. So we decided to push on, once again, through the night to the south. But first we'd have a meal at a good hotel. We were in somewhat scruffy khaki drill, not having anything else, and were told at the hotel that we could not be admitted without dinner-jackets and that there was an extra charge as it was a dance night! We asked them if they realised that they would be overrun by the enemy in a matter of days and settled for a two-course meal in an ante-chamber. Meanwhile Dutch diners and dancers were turning up in their evening dresses.

From Batavia, local men had been quite gaily leaving their wives and daughters behind. I saw a local bank manager with a belt under his shirt filled with bonds of some sort, leaving his wife and family to an unknown future. I have often wondered what happened to our attractive plotter girls; I hope they came through safely.

Our four carloads duly arrived at the port in the early morning and were relieved to find the *Zandaam* due to sail that night. It was, of course, crammed full, mostly with civilians, both Dutch and British, some of whom had come by various means from Singapore. Every cabin was occupied and we were told we could sleep on the deck. We had brought a blanket each with us and Barclay had the cunning to nip down below, unseen, and pinch two pillows which we hid under our blankets.

The previous day two ships, one the *City of Manchester*, had sailed and been sunk immediately by Japanese submarines lying off the harbour. Our Captain, therefore, waited until nightfall in the hope of avoiding a similar fate; but night brought the brightest full moon I have ever seen, with not a trace of cloud. A ship with the high superstructure of the *Zandaam* would be seen ten miles away.

Before we sailed, the last British warship in those waters, the destroyer *Stronghold*, came alongside and the Captain shouted through a megaphone that he would do an anti-submarine search ahead of us. This produced shouts of approval from our thoroughly anxious passengers. As senior officer aboard, I went to the bridge and suggested to the Dutch Captain that he should turn right or left immediately after leaving the harbour mouth along the coast, keeping the ship's high silhouette against the dark, high tree-covered hills, before venturing into the moonlit open sea. He replied, 'Ach, dat is a goot idea: I vill do dat.' Accordingly we did, in fact, turn sharply and with a man on the line calling out the depths, we crept along slowly and carefully for an hour or so.

In the meantime the luckless *Stronghold* went straight ahead and was torpedoed and sunk immediately. Obviously, we could not go and help, or undoubtedly we would have suffered the same fate.

Much later the same night we lay down on the deck—and how hard a deck is. Before this, however, a charming lady, walking nervously round the deck, eventually came up to us and said, 'May I join you there? I daren't go below to my cabin.'

She had come all the way from Singapore, had been torpedoed once off Sumatra and picked up from the sea by another ship and brought on to Java so, understandably, wanted to stay on deck. So down she came between Barclay and me, and it was a bit of a shock to wake from a fitful doze to find a blonde head beside me on the pillow.

The following day we picked up a boat-load of passengers from two torpedoed ships, who were lucky since they had been making for Java. I scanned the ocean nervously while we slowed to a stop to take them aboard. We had set out for Ceylon, but on the second day we realised by the sun that we were going south, having been ordered to alter course for Australia.

Twice a day we formed into a long queue and filed past the pantry window where we were issued out with a large, quite nasty sandwich with a fatty, greasy bacon interior, and a cup of tea. Sometimes there was an orange or an apple. Five days of this grew very monotonous but we were, of course, mighty grateful for it. The blonde head was most delighted when our course was changed for Fremantle instead of Ceylon, as she had sent her two sons to Perth, for which Fremantle is the port, when it became clear that Singapore would fall. She did, in fact, rejoin them soon after our arrival in Australia.

The night we got in I gave a dinner party in the Australia

Hotel to those of us, but including the blonde, who had planned the yacht trip.

I rang the Headquarters in Melbourne to report our arrival and Air Marshal Sir Charles Burnett said, 'I'm so glad you have arrived, you know all about Home Defence. We know nothing and the Jap is on the way. We have seen photos of W.A.A.F.s sitting round tables with headphones on, but we don't know who they are talking to.'

I said, 'I can tell you that!'

15

Australasian interlude

It was now the middle of March 1942 and I was back into the air again, this time as a passenger in a D.C.2 of Australian National Airways. A whole day of boring flat country with four refuelling stops brought us to Melbourne.

On the recommendation of the C.-in-C., I moved into the Melbourne Club where I was very comfortable, and set about getting some uniform and clothes fit for me to stay and organise their Home Defence system. For the next four months I flew back to Perth and two or three times up the east coast and on into New Guinea, commandeering houses or having Operations Rooms built to my design, and arranging for an Observer Corps, radar stations and communications. The work was given the highest priority as it was considered the Japanese would continue their successful advance down the S.W. Pacific islands to Australia and New Zealand.

On many trips I flew Royal Australian Air Force aircraft—Wirraways, a Fairchild, Miles Falcon and for two long trips to New Guinea an American P-40 Kittyhawk.

The P-40 Kittyhawk had a good cruising speed and a change of clothing and washing gear could be squeezed in, but it was, of course, only a single-seater. On one trip Wing Commander Biggar accompanied me in another P-40. We spent the night at the Australian Club in Sydney having an early call and leaving Mascot aerodrome about 06.00 hrs.

We arrived at Brisbane for breakfast to be met by an anxious officer asking what had happened. We asked him what he was talking about. It transpired that aircraft had been sent out to scour the sea for a mother submarine that was assumed to have towed in a number of miniature subs which had, in fact, got into Sydney harbour that night. Guns and torpedoes had been fired, depth-charges dropped and much excitement caused in the harbour, below the famous bridge which I could see from my club window. Having got used now to such sounds neither of us had awakened and being called at 04.30 hrs before any news bulletins were given out we were blissfully unaware. Those at Brisbane were amazed, having hoped to receive dramatic accounts from us.

For two or three nights at Port Moresby in New Guinea we dodged the large bomber mosquitoes, which I am sure were escorted by smaller, fighter, ones. These affected us far more than the Japanese, who bombed the harbour. I have never seen such voracious mosquitoes though I don't think there were any of the Anopheles Malaria type. In the evening, if we left the safe proximity of a pink lamp to venture outside, they swooped, humming and stinging!

On one occasion for this trip I used a Falcon Six with Pilot Officer Soilleaux as passenger, which took longer but was still a pleasant journey. The coast was mile after mile of wonderful beach with great rollers coming in from about a quarter of a mile—ideal for surfing—and leaving an area of high, very fine spray, known as 'smoke'. It was wonderful to fly a few feet above this beach with barely a soul on it and even to fly into the 'smoke', though not very kind to the aeroplane or mechanics who had to clean it later. After my period of enforced grounding I was able thoroughly to enjoy this flying, getting in about 150 hours of varied flying in four months. During this time the Americans arrived and were taking over command of all Pacific operations, so I handed over my not-quite-finished commitment to them.

The Commanding General asked me to report on why their squadron in New Guinea was not being successful against the frequent Japanese bombing raids, so I visited their main strip not many miles from Port Moresby. I found the camp in a state of filth, tents with unmade camp beds, food tins and cans of all sorts lying about on the ground attracting millions of flies, and unshaven officers and airmen who, being new to a war, considered they had to be 'tough' to fight. I watched a section of two P-39 fighters scrambled . . . it took fifteen minutes to become airborne. After the two minutes for a complete squadron in the Battle of Britain, I was shaken.

Later the usual twenty-seven Jap bombers came over, when the P-39s, who had the height over them and were good aeroplanes, carried out one dive without any effect on the bombers, and carried on diving down to ground level in order to avoid being shot at! I told the Colonel on the spot and later the General that what was wrong was nothing but bad morale, caused by slovenliness and 'dirt'. I asked how could a fighter pilot go with any confidence or encouragement when seen off by unshaven and dirty airmen. My comments were not at all popular and I don't know if they had any result at all as I soon left the country!

I saw the Japs have some really bad luck—which was remarkably good luck for us of course. There was an ammunition ship in Port Moresby harbour full of shells, bombs and ammunition of all sizes and explosives, which the enemy must have known well. They sent a formation of twenty-seven bombers which formed into a big V for the actual bombing. I was standing on high ground overlooking the harbour and saw some very accurate aiming by the leader, on whose orders all bombs were dropped simultaneously. The ship was completely obscured by spray from the bursting bombs but not one single hit was registered, as the ship was precisely in the centre of the 'Vee'.

At Brisbane I was talking in the local club to a young American pilot who said he was not accustomed to seeing the equivalent of their Brigadiers flying themselves around the country in Kittyhawks, but then, he supposed, the average Brigadier was a good deal older than the British Air Commodore. When I asked what the average was he replied, 'Oh, they're pretty old, about 45!' Unfortunately Wing Commander Biggar told him my age.

Air Commodore Goddard, Chief of Air Staff in New Zealand, heard I was leaving Australia on handing over to the Americans so he, in turn, asked the Air Ministry if I could go there also to do the same work with their defence system. Back again in a comfortable Empire flying boat, this time of Tasman Airways from Sydney to Auckland, New Zealand, in a little under eight hours; not very rapid, but spacious and gracious.

I took with me Squadron Leader Brooker who had been helping me since Sumatra—a quiet, reliable and excellent officer who had done well in the Battle of Britain, Singapore, Sumatra and Java. In a series of hops first in an Airspeed Oxford and later in a De Havilland Dragon Rapide—in which we picked up Air Commodore Goddard who welcomed me at New Plymouth—we flew to Rongotai, at Wellington, the last bit being at a few feet around the coastline under very low cloud.

I toured for several weeks to fix up a control and reporting organisation in much the same way as in Australia, but after doing this in North and South Islands, I eventually stayed for nine months, as Deputy Chief of Air Staff to Goddard, who had to be away for considerable periods with Admiral Nimitz, the American C.-in-C. in the Pacific Theatre. Goddard needed a Senior Officer to leave behind to supervise the training, and from the political angle. In all, a very enjoyable time to come, with plenty of work and plenty of flying over the islands and the Pacific.

New Zealand is so different from Australia to fly over; the latter being mostly vast areas of desert and gum trees—mostly dead skeletons—only relieved by the marvellous coastal strip, but the former all mountains and luxuriant countryside. Australia is usually calm to fly over, but New Zealand usually bumpy when flying at the heights flown in 1942.

I saw more of the country than most New Zealanders, having stood at its extreme northern tip of the North Island, down both east and west sides of both to nearly the extreme south of the South Island. In New Zealand there were such old aircraft friends as the Whitney Straight, D.H. Rapide biplane, Vega Gull, and Harvards.

On several occasions I visited the aerodromes at Whenuapai, Ohakia, Omaha (Blenheim), Woodburn, Nelson, Taieri (Dunedin), Wigram (Christchurch), Gisborne, Napier, Paraparamu, Tauranga, Seagrove, Waipapakuri, New Plymouth, Masterton, Levin, Hoasti, Hokitika and Palmerston North, all flown from the Wellington base at Rongotai—an interesting little strip of a landing-ground which had to be approached on almost every occasion from a saddle of hill with the hill rising higher on each side, and with its consequent 'sink' at the ground having come over and through. An attractive challenge on every landing! In addition to this interesting flying I had two trips—as a passenger in a Hudson—up into the Pacific where the R.N.Z.A.F. had two or three squadrons supporting the Americans.

The Pacific is very big—the islands are very small and the navigation had to be exceedingly good. There were no mechanical radio aids and navigators had to work manually and mentally. Those from the R.N.Z.A.F. were first class and I never had any worry—in fact we had to lend twenty of them for three months to the Americans who were having terrible losses. They went with their bombers and reconnaissance aeroplanes and taught the practical working to their half-trained navigators with very satisfactory results.

Fiji is a very beautiful island with two aerodromes at Suva and Nandi. We had fighters for a time at the latter. On my two Pacific trips I went again to Fiji and also to Tonga Tontouta, Noumea, New Caledonia and Plaines des Gaiacs, all very lovely islands, particularly Fiji and Tonga with every imaginable flowering shrub and tree, and bright green in between—franjipani, hibiscus, banana and pineapple, etc.

At Nandi we built some dispersal points for the protection of the fighters, but the freshly dug brown earth mounds showed up seriously in the midst of the luscious green all round, so some small shoots about six inches high of pineapple were planted a foot or two apart and in only a few months there were healthy bushes, with the dispersals rendered invisible from above. And in just a few months more every bush was producing small but delicious pineapples. The Americans sent

Dakotas over from some of the other islands and loaded them up with fruit from these bushes which could easily be spared.

On one of my trips up into the Pacific I visited an American General and his staff on an island to discuss the use of R.N.Z.A.F. squadrons in support of United States Forces in their coming island-hopping strategy commencing with the invasion of Guadalcanal. This was very hush-hush and the strictest security was enforced. During lunch in a house which they had made as a mess with a beautiful view over the coast and sea, the General made me shrink with horror as he said, in front of the English-speaking local waiters, 'It was a wonderful sight yesterday when the convoy of troopships and all their escort sailed past here, close inshore, on their way to Guadalcanal.' The landing date was still two days ahead!

At Noumea an R.N.Z.A.F. squadron was carrying out anti-submarine searches in a fan-shaped sweep centred on a lighthouse about a mile offshore. The Americans, on the same aerodrome, were impressed by the fact that the N.Z. Hudsons disappeared on a straight line and about an hour later came into view again from their new heading but on a dead straight line for the lighthouse then, on a further diverging course, disappearing to reappear once again from a still wider angle, but still straight towards the lighthouse. They were so impressed by this accurate navigation that they asked us to lend them twenty navigators for a few months to show theirs how to do it! This was done, and two navigators, one of each nationality, travelled in their Fortresses and Liberators for a time, and the alarming number of losses through failing to find small island locations without radio aids, fell rapidly, and all the N.Z. navigators returned safely in the end.

At their mess on this island I was amused at breakfast one morning to find a charming lady sitting beside me—not in uniform of any sort. I asked her what her duties were, and she replied, 'Oh, I haven't got any duties, I'm just here to boost up Colonel X's morale'!

16

Round the world

Eight and a half hours is a long time in the back of a small twin-engined aeroplane over the Pacific—even trusting the navigator implicitly, it is a great relief to see a small speck appear in front! It is boring with the sea, sea, and nothing but sea to look at, but did give me the chance to write letters. I kept writing these from the various countries I had passed through but it was not until April 9th in Australia that I received the first word from my wife since I had left in January. This was a cable, and I felt much better having established communication again. The remainder of my old No. 226 Group had returned to the United Kingdom from Australia in the middle of April. Squadron Leader Brooker, who had been accompanying me, took over command of a R.N.Z.A.F. fighter squadron.

I had an amusing and satisfying flight to the station at Ohakea on one occasion in a Harvard. The C.O., considering it a good occasion to test his ground control and interception capability, sent his chief instructor with a small formation to intercept me some ten to fifteen miles from base. Sure enough they brought this off and I thought I'd oblige further. So, instead of just flying steadily on, I took violent evasive action and the leader, also flying a Harvard, started a lusty dogfight. After a time, I got firmly on his tail and 'shot him down' without any doubt. Having achieved my success I waggled my wings and the remainder fell in formation and escorted me in to the aerodrome. I felt that the old man Air Commodore hadn't done himself any harm and would be listened to more easily! One of their formation was in a Spitfire and he claimed he had 'got' me when I was on his leader's tail, so all were satisfied.

One day I flew a Vega Gull from Wellington to Christchurch in the South Island with a Colonel, Major and Corporal as passengers. We crossed the Tasman Straits in very low cloud and rain and after some ten minutes we hadn't sighted the coast ahead, the officers got fidgety, so I asked them to pass the map. I then peered over the side and said, 'Oh, it's all right, there's that wave so we're on course O.K.' This conveyed to them that at least I wasn't worried, and in due course the coastline appeared where I expected. As the weather also cleared up we had a very pleasant trip down the coast to the aerodrome at Wigram. Here I found in command 'Grid' Caldwell with whom I had been in France in No. 60 Squadron during the First World War, and was very pleased to see him again.

I was asked to take the salute at a big parade at New Plymouth at the north of the South Island and flew there in a Harvard, where I found a vast turn-out with troops, two or three bands, girl drum majorettes and junior formations, before a big crowd and the mayor and local dignitaries on a dais, where I joined them. The mayor then said that I was advertised to 'open' it as well as just take the salute, so I asked my neighbour on my right what 'IT' was . . . what was I to open? He said he didn't know and passed on the question to his neighbour, and so it went on up to the back row and all round until it came to the mayor who was beside me on the left. He, in turn, said he didn't know either, but considered 'Fête' would be better than 'Fair'! In due course I duly opened the Fête in a few 'well-chosen words'. It was an amusing start to an extremely smart and impressive parade and march past.

During Victor Goddard's absence in the Pacific I had to attend in the Parliament building during debates in case the Prime Minister had to get particulars for a reply to any R.N.Z.A.F. question. This was interesting and—luckily—there was only one query, which I was able to answer on the spot.

Early in my time in New Zealand I was living in the Wellington Club and had only just gone to bed when I heard an ominous rumbling coming nearer and the room began to shake. I leaped out of bed and opened the door and stood in the doorway with the idea that if the building collapsed I would be protected by the frame. The lights swung, things fell off the tables and it was very shaky—I looked across the landing and there were all the other residents in their doorways the same as I. The housekeeper came round shortly with tea, which was very welcome. The club being built entirely of wood, as are the vast majority of Wellington houses for this reason, remained standing which I am sure it would not had it been of brick construction. No less than 1,500 brick chimneys came down in this shock which was the worst the town had experienced for many years. In spite of all these falling chimney stacks there was only one fatality and even this was not caused by falling bricks or masonry but by a gas leak caused by a broken pipe.

I had seven days' leave in the middle of my tour and flew up to Tauranga on the east coast of the North Island, taking with me Christopher Holland-Martin of the Governor General's staff. We had a pleasant time playing golf every day and also visiting the famous geysers and boiling mud at Rotorua.

Air Commodore Nevill of the R.N.Z.A.F. had been to England to get up to date, and on return took over from me as D.C.A.S. and arrangements were made for me to go to the United States to negotiate for more aircraft for the R.N.Z.A.F. After nine very full months I went by sea to San Francisco, the only bit of my round-the-world trip not by air.

After a night in San Francisco—'I guessed you were English because of your funny accent'!—I went by airline to Los Angeles and San Diego to see the Lockheed and Consolidated aircraft plants and their latest products. I was shown round Los Angeles by one of the wealthiest on the many wealthy locals, with a Wing Commander Wells, a New Zealander, who was returning to the war from which he had been on home leave, having done very well in the Battle of Britain and later.

The poor Wing Commander was feeling very poorly with an attack of 'flu and wanted to get to a bed more than anything, but our host wouldn't hear of it and showed us Earl Carol's

Vanities, a splendid cabaret show on a grand scale, and then on to some night club 'where all the cinema stars go'. We eventually had something to eat in the early hours of the morning after a great number of double Scotches. We did see two or three recognisable faces, but by then could scarcely care less, and I persuaded our host to take us back to our hotel, in order to get poor suffering Wells to bed.

On the way, however, he said he badly wanted to show us his house, but having firmly dissuaded him, he turned back after half an hour or so to say, 'It's no use, I've just *got* to show you my house!' In we went past the inevitable large swimming pool into his bar, a 'little' room about 40 feet in length; he proceeded to dish out yet more double whiskies, where he, fortunately, passed out himself! We then persuaded another guest to pinch the car and drive us to our hotel. Surprisingly, Wells was much better the following morning!

I was amazed to find the huge Consolidated plant completely concealed under an elaborate netting camouflage cover on which were built roads, trees, houses and even cars to deceive somebody! When I asked who, they said the Japanese. The fact that they were some 4,000 miles away and that there was a huge Pacific fleet in between to stop any aircraft carrier getting anywhere near range didn't worry them a bit; they had obviously had great fun making it and since it had cost 'X' million dollars it was, therefore, a good thing!

At San Diego we spent two nights in the 'Coloured Supplement Hotel'. Everything was beautiful: climate, swimming pool, tennis courts, golf course, beach, food and accommodation. Beauteous damsels strolling about in brief shorts, tanned the same all over—it was difficult to imagine that quite a war was going on elsewhere.

The second evening we were lent a large Buick to cross the border into Mexico where silk stockings could be obtained and we returned with them wrapped round the waist and inside our hats feeling desperate smugglers! Eventually they reached my wife's legs.

By night we flew in a D.C.3 over to Washington with refuelling stops at Tucson, El Paso, Dallas, Memphis and Nashville, a long and tiring trip leading up to several visits to the Navy building and the Pentagon, where details of an aircraft order were argued out—taking about a week before flying on to New York where I had been asked to give a talk to about 300 veterans of the First World War. These were a splendid audience and keen to find out what had happened to this or that aerodrome in Britain where they had served, and what were the differences and similarities of First and Second Wars. Many double Scotches had to be drunk with one after another afterwards.

Then by train to Montreal, the air trip having to be cancelled owing to heavy snow. After one night a dozen of us climbed into the belly of a B-24 Liberator and flew to Halifax where we refuelled and left by night to cross the Atlantic. We lay on straw, crosswise, head to feet, and with a good wind behind us did, in fact, beat the record to date for the coast to coast crossing.

We passed by the north coast of Ireland soon after dawn and a young American Corporal looking out of the one small window exclaimed, 'Gee! Ain't it green!' And it was; it looked so fresh and clean after the dusty brown of American grass. It was a welcome sight preceding our landing at Prestwick, where I was lucky to find a Wellington going to Hendon. So I finished my complete circuit of the world with almost 400 hours of flying time added to my log-book. Where would I be sent? I might have guessed; back to Duty Air Commodore 'down the hole' in the Operations Room at Fighter Command Headquarters at Bentley Priory!

Five troglodyte months covering the summer of 1943 went by here during which time I only flew—between watches—on ten occasions using a Vega Gull, Hurricane, Proctor and Oxford. Then, to my joy, I was posted to command No. 13 Fighter Group in Scotland.

Up to this time there had been two Fighter Groups in the north, Nos. 13 and 14, each commanded by an Air Vice-Marshal. Now they had combined, with No. 14 H.Q. staff disbanded and buildings closed. The double-sized group with H.Q.

at Inverness was then commanded by one Air Commodore! They had been having a lazy time, just waiting to intercept anything that might materialise and the pilots were bored, so they were delighted when I started some offensive raids into the Norwegian coast where Mosquitoes shot down several German aircraft, mostly on training flights. My eldest son who had joined the R.A.F. was, as an A.C.2, waiting to go to the U.S.A. for pilot training. He was not doing anything so I managed to get him to come up (as my orderly) for a short time. He came with me in a Proctor to various stations in the Group which he enjoyed and so, of course, did I.

Stations in the Group were at Longman (Inverness), Peterhead, Turnhouse (Edinburgh), Errol (Dundee), Kinnell, Skeabrae in the Orkneys; being winter there was plenty of snow to dodge. I had a good Spitfire to do my single-seater visits and went to Turnhouse several times as we had a Planning Committee there to plan the invasion of Norway, for which I was designated the A.O.C. working with the 3rd Division, with whom we carried out some preliminary exercises in the cold and the snow near Brechin over two or three days and nights.

However, this was not to be as one evening, after only two months with the Group, the Air Member for Personnel at the Air Ministry rang me up and said, 'I know you've only been back home a short time so I will fully understand if you say no, and you may say this if you feel like it; but I remember you saying you weren't very fond of the Japs and I can give you the opportunity of getting your own back.'

Well, in wartime, there is only one answer to that kind of question. I replied, 'Right, sir, where do I go and when?'

So I found that I had less than a week to hand over my group, get kitted up for the East again and get down to Poole harbour to fly out once again to the Far East, this time to Imphal on the Burma border. I had only just got my wife up to Scotland but, fortunately, we had not yet got a house and were in a hotel in Inverness.

This time on the night of February 2nd, 1944, I flew in a Sunderland flying boat to Gibraltar, thence to Jerba and Cairo, where I saw Air Marshal Park, and so on to Habbaniyah and

Bahrain to Karachi. At Delhi I met Victor Goddard again, also John Baker and Bill Williams. The following morning I met the 'Supremo', Lord Louis Mountbatten, the C.-in-C. General Auchinleck, and had lunch with the American General Stratemeyer and dinner in the senior officers' mess with Jim Crowe and Freddie Guest. The next day Bill Williams sent me in his B-25 Mitchell to Calcutta where I was put up for the night by 'Tog' Mellersh, A.O.C. of No. 223 Bomber Group.

On the 16th in another B-25, I went to 3rd T.A.F. Headquarters at Comilla, met the Air Commander once again (Air Marshal Sir John Baldwin) and on to Imphal, which struck me as a delightful place, and thoroughly cold at night. Here I took over No. 221 Group from a somewhat disgruntled Rowley, who had had his sailing orders at very short notice, and he left the next day after lunch, and I started in, rather groping my way with a lot of strangers, and trying to learn all the strange names all round my 'parish' and country over which the Group aircraft operated.

17

Burma battle

The Imphal Valley in which was Group Headquarters and No. 170 Wing and six airstrips is a very beautiful place. It is a valley of about 35 miles north to south and about 18 miles across at its widest; the valley itself is about 2,600 feet high with surrounding hills of up to some 6,000 feet, with larger ones in the background up to nearly 10,000. The hills are covered with jungle, and the bowl of the valley almost entirely with paddy fields which are usually green and thereby give a pleasing aspect.

The Group Headquarters' accommodation was all of the local 'basha' construction, bamboo with a thatch roof and bamboo leaf walls, usually covered with a smear of mud to keep out the cold winds of the winter and the mosquitoes of summer. These bashas were cut into the hillside in a series of terraces, and the A.O.C.'s bungalow was a particularly fine one in a good position near the officers' mess. This had the added luxury of asbestos sheet lining and a corrugated iron roof under the thatch, with a large fireplace. The accommodation consisted of one decent-sized living-room, two small bedrooms and two small bathrooms, one of each of the latter being occupied by the Senior Air Staff Office. The bath was only of the hip variety, never filled more than two or three inches deep, owing to the shortage of water and the difficulty in heating it.

From the bungalow verandah there was a view across the valley, and it was always delightful to sit there and watch the effect of the sunset on the hills and clouds opposite, though the sun was actually setting behind the hill on which the bungalow was built.

The jungle on the hill behind the bungalow, mess and offices was quite thick, and large numbers of monkeys entertained us frequently, swinging from tree to tree and coming very close to the buildings. There were the little 'barrel-organ' type—pleasant little animals—also the larger, longer-bodied, rather stiff-legged variety, and also baboons.

The Group covered an area approximating to a triangle with points in London, Devon and Yorkshire. Some squadrons were in the Imphal Valley and the Surma Valley about eighty miles to the west where there were several other strips and two Wings, and where it was much hotter and stickier during the summer and monsoon period. In the Brahmaputra Valley to the north there was another Wing with four strips also hotter and stickier than the Imphal Valley, and was frequently difficult to get at owing to the clouds on the high mountains.

Alongside Group Headquarters worked with General Scoones of IV Corps and with General Wingate in connection with his forthcoming long range penetration operation behind the Japanese lines. They were two very different characters and it was always interesting to go from one to the other.

One of my units was No. 1 (Indian Air Force) Squadron commanded by Squadron Leader Arjan Singh, a very good type who led the Squadron well in the air and also had it well organised on the ground. A dinner with them was followed by a concert of their local turns and also by some of the Manipuri dancers, Imphal being in the state of Manipur. These dances are quite attractive and symbolical, hands and arms have movements of great significance, which was, of course, unknown to such members of the audience as myself. But their purely local type of dancing with their musical accompaniment on a sort of harmonica, flat on the floor, is quite entertaining for a spell.

Round about 24th February, there were definite signs of the Jap livening up a bit on the far bank of the Chindwin river, which runs approximately north to south about 55 miles east of Imphal at its nearest point. Accordingly, I stepped up the tempo of our operations and bombed and shot up places where the Jap was considered to be collecting or crossing the river. On one of these we put three Vengeance dive-bomber squadrons and three Hurribomber squadrons—which was quite a concentration—so I went out in my Hurricane to watch, and saw early in my tour the difficulties that the squadrons had to contend with in that country, where results of attacks were hidden by the density of the jungle. I emptied all my guns into the target area just to feel I was getting a little of my own back for the days in Singapore, Sumatra and Java.

During this time Wingate's 3rd Indian Division long range penetration was building up and I had frequent meetings with him to discuss details. He was a very interesting character and, being in his early forties, young for a Major-General. He was growing a masterly beard which he affected at times of jungle penetration! He was also the only wearer of a topee in this part of the world, and being short, wearing a beard, a topee, a D.S.O. and two Bars, and being a bunch of compressed energy, he was very refreshing company. I got on well with him and was exceedingly sorry when he was later killed in a night air crash.

At the end of February I had a two-day tour round the rear part of the Group, going to Kumbirgram, Silchar, Patharkandi and back to Kumbirgram on the first day, then on to Dimapur for lunch, returning to Imphal before night. On this last leg one has to fly over mountains of almost exactly 10,000 feet and there are some fine views, provided there are not storms and clouds to make it rather frightening. On the next day I went to my most forward airfield, Tamu, over the Burma border, being used as an emergency landing-ground and as a forward and suitable base for an early warning radar. There were at this isolated position only a few radar personnel and an R.A.F. Regiment detachment to guard them; the Japs were already close and we soon had to pull our people out.

The night of March 5th/6th was the start of the Wingate long range penetration operation and the gliders with airfield construction engineers were towed over the valley from the Surma Valley. The majority found the right area in the moonlight, but owing to lack of experience and wrong ideas on the part of the Americans concerned, many were killed or lost by trying to tow two gliders instead of one behind each Dakota over ranges of mountains, by night, though much gallant work was done by the remainder.

I flew back to Hailakandi and then to Rajyeswarpur (called by the Americans Lalaghat) to a conference with General Slim, Fourteenth Army, General Wingate, 3rd Indian Division, General Old of United States Air Transport Command, and Colonel Cochran of the United States First Air Commando Force.

The conference was called to decide whether we should proceed or not with the plan owing to the mess-up and casualties of the previous night. From reports to hand things looked black, but during discussions, a wireless message came through from Broadway—the name given to the strip being constructed about 100 miles behind the Japanese lines—that it would be usable by Dakotas that night. So it was decided to proceed, and the rest of the fly-over the next week or so went with conspicuous success and virtually no further accidents.

Two days later the Japs reacted by bringing a considerable number of aircraft up to Shwebo, obviously in order to attack the strip at Broadway or the points of emplaning in the Imphal and Surma Valleys. So all our available aircraft were turned on to attack their strip at Shwebo, including No. 5 Squadron which went out from Sapam after dark to do a low strafing attack with cannon-fire. I went to Sapam to watch their return. They came in satisfactorily and reported many fires on Shwebo aerodrome, and it was considered that through the combined attacks of ourselves and the Americans the Japs lost 40-odd aircraft.

Later that night I went to Tulihal, where I witnessed one of the most dramatic things I have ever seen. Tulihal was a strip 4,000 by 200 yards; but being a kutcha strip was therefore very dusty in dry weather. In the centre, to each side were arrayed some 50 or 60 Dakotas, looking very impressive in the moonlight.

Behind each aircraft was a post bearing a numbered placard; to each aircraft a certain number of troops and a number of mules was allotted and one could see a file of 12 to 15 silent

Gurkhas, moving across to their allotted number, followed by three mules. They were carrying machine-guns and rifles, packs and rations, and the mules were driven up a ramp into the sides of the Dakotas—occasionally with trouble from a very stubborn one. These three mules took up the space forward, side by side in an especially constructed bamboo 'stable'. Behind these the troops emplaned, expressionless, and it was impossible to tell whether they were excited, pleased or frightened.

At its allotted time, a jeep would drive in front of the aircraft, signal to it, the engines would start, and it would taxi out, and after other signals would take off into the night. Being a 4,000-yard strip with the aircraft located in the centre, two took off simultaneously in opposite directions. Twelve would go off in this manner in succession, then there would be a pause while the dust subsided and twelve would return from their first load, having done approximately 300 miles and landing on a very small rough strip in the middle of the jungle in enemy territory. By the time the dust had cleared, another twelve would be loaded and would take off, and so it went on all night.

I watched this for two or three nights. I saw a British soldier one night trying to lead his stubborn mule into the aircraft; he didn't shout, swear, kick or pull it, but led it right round the aircraft back to the ramp again, stroked its neck and nose, and said, 'Don't you want to go for a ride in this lovely kite?' Whereupon, the mule walked into the aircraft with no trouble at all! I had a feeling that this Cockney soldier was probably far more frightened than the mule. After all, it was probably his first flight in an aircraft, and at night, flying over mountain ranges to land in enemy-occupied territory.

About this time we were starting in the Imphal Valley to 'Get into Boxes'. The Jap was advancing from the south, from the south-east and east towards our valley and I had a conference with Scoones—the General commanding IV Corps—when he asked me if I would remove the Group H.Q. and most of the units from the valley and operate further back. I told him I had done enough retreating from the Japs in the past and didn't intend to do any more and wanted to stay put, for I was perfectly confident that we were able to beat the Jap thoroughly.

Accordingly, we prepared defensive positions on every airstrip and Headquarters. Bunkers and slit trenches had to be dug and prepared, rations and ammunition laid on, and airmen and officers given extra combat training.

Our reasonably comfortable domestic sites, a mile or so from the airstrips, were given up, while the personnel moved into uncomfortable positions, but in great heart, and determined to defend their aircraft and themselves. This was a most unusual and interesting phase, as I don't think the Air Force has ever lived in quite the same conditions anywhere, finishing up by being completely surrounded by the Jap at very short range indeed, and the only supplies being those that were flown in. About March 9th General Wingate asked me if I could possibly get some fighters up to Broadway to defend it, as Colonel Cochran and his American fighters had flown out. He knew it would not be long before the Japs got there; so on the 11th, after much preparation and many conferences, we got a flight of No. 81 Squadron with Spitfire VIIIs flown in, and on the night of the 12th I went out myself to see how they were settling in and conditions in general.

The following morning was when the Japs finally did find the place, and we were attacked for 50 minutes with bombs and gun-fire from about 40 to 50 Oscars and Zeros. The newly arrived Spitfires jumped into the air, though with little warning, so that the last one to take off was caught by the enemy at a disadvantage and was unfortunately shot down into the jungle. The remaining four, however, put up an epic fight and each shot down one of the enemy. As the anti-aircraft guns also got one, the Jap lost a far higher percentage than they could ever have imagined, as I do not think they expected to find Bofors guns in reasonable numbers, and certainly not Spitfires, flown by very able and determined pilots, in the heart of their own territory.

Being heavily outnumbered, there were times when these Spitfire pilots found about two of the enemy on their tail, which they could not shake off. A manœuvre was evolved by several of them in co-operation with the Army. This was to dive down across the strip, followed by the Zeros, into the field of fire of the Bofors guns, who would shoot them off the tail of the Spitfires: even if not shot down, the evasive action gave the Spitfires their chance to turn the tables and get on their tails.

I started off by standing behind a teak tree and then found bullets were coming from all sides, so managed to get along to a slit trench which I shared with a Gurkha. I was entertained by his immobility; it was impossible to tell whether he was frightened, angry, or just bored. He would pop up every now and then when the opportunity offered and fire with his rifle. When the attack tailed off and I wanted to get a better view, I left the trench and gave him a friendly salute of thanks, saying 'Thank you for your trench'. He just looked mildly surprised, and perhaps thought that I was obviously as mad as most Englishmen!

The following morning before light I returned as a passenger in an American Dakota and considered myself very lucky to have witnessed the first big attack, followed by three or four false alarms, of course, and I had met all the people concerned at Broadway. I flew the Dakota most of the way back but handed over to the owner who made a very nice landing at Kangla.

Early the following morning General Wingate was round to get my impressions on Broadway and the air defence of the area, and was as enthusiastic as usual. I had another hour or two with him the following day, which was refreshing after a visit to General Scoones of IV Corps, who was understandably rather gloomy due to the retreat of the 17th Division up the Tiddim road in particular, and withdrawal all round in general.

18

Battle of the Boxes

About this time we were having frequent air raids by the Jap. On the night of March 15th/16th four came over, of which one was shot down by our Beaufighters, followed by a day and a night raid on the 16th. We got two down in the morning, but at night a stick of bombs fell along slit trenches causing 28 army casualties.

On the 17th Jack Baldwin (Air Marshal Sir John Baldwin's Third Tactical Air Force) came on a short visit with Lady Trefusis Forbes, the 'Queen Bee' W.A.A.F. She was in good form and not in so much of a hurry to get out of the action zone as some of her escort. On this day we had a sad loss at Broadway: the young C.O. of No. 81 Squadron, W. M. Whitamore, after having shot down a Jap fighter, was shot down and killed himself. This was a great blow as he was a real 'Fighter Boy', had done well in the Battle of Britain and in North Africa, having shot down seven German and two Jap aircraft, and commanded a squadron with great dash and ability at the age of twenty-one. We all felt his loss very much.

At this time all officers and airmen in the Group, both at Headquarters, the Wing Headquarters, squadrons and units, were feverishly digging trenches, making bunkers and generally siting defences and doing extra training with rifles, machine-guns, revolvers and other arms in order to defend ourselves when IV Corps would have 'advanced beyond' us!

Most of the strips or airfields had native-built basha accommodation of reasonable comfort, about a mile or two from the strip for bomb-dodging reasons, but this meant leaving the aircraft too open to sabotage and ground attack generally, so we had to bring everyone in to defence positions in a 'Box' at some suitable point or points right alongside. This meant that the pilots after a hard day's flying with two or three sorties over the usual mountains, and the airmen after working feverishly to keep the aircraft in the air from before dawn to after dark, would then have to roll themselves up in ground sheets and sleep in the somewhat inexpertly made 'Bunker'—a wide trench roofed over with wood and tarpaulin.

We used to have 25 per cent strength on the alert all night which, in conjunction with patrols by the R.A.F. Regiment (who also manned static posts on hill-tops around), proved insufficient on one particular occasion, when the Jap did get right in among the aircraft by night and destroy six with small bombs in spite of having been seen and fired at. On other occasions the airmen were glad to be in the trenches, particularly on two separate nights at Palel, when the Jap tried to capture the place, and bullets were flying somewhat aimlessly about for several hours. During this time only one airman had the extreme bad luck to be killed, as he was caught outside his trench and was, apparently, shot by one of our own Indian troops in the neighbourhood.

From March 19th onwards for a few days the 5th Division were flown in from the Arakan. The transport aircraft were pouring in all day long with troops, jeeps, guns and mules in big numbers. This was a big consolation to us to feel a whole division had been added to our local defence.

On the evening of the 24th General Wingate came to see me, having been flown round the three strips in his long-range patrol area (behind the Jap lines), to discuss the future fighter defence, radar cover and associated matters. I gave him the last drop of real Scotch whisky that I had in a bottle, as he looked tired after a long day. I was very glad I had done this, as immediately after he left they took off into the dark to fly back to the Surma Valley, and for reasons not properly explained, they crashed, and all were killed on the way. They probably flew into one of the terrible clouds unseen in the dark and lost control in the turbulence. I was, therefore, the last to see him alive, with the exception of the crew who were killed with him, and I was most sorry. Although he was 'mad' and had strange ideas and did many things in strange ways, he certainly was 'offensive minded', enthusiastic and optimistic.

The Japs were getting nearer every day towards the end of the month and I had to evacuate Kangla airstrip, pull in two of the radar installations, all of which was loss to efficiency. We kept on knocking down two or three Japs every day or so as they came over on raids, and were gradually getting the measure of them, watching them get more and more frightened of the Spitfires, until eventually when they saw them their main idea was to avoid them.

On March 30th the Dimapur road was cut, so we were then in a state of siege. Our only line of communication, one road (no rail) and one track for about 70 miles over the mountains to Silchar, were cut by the enemy at the same time.

I wrote out an 'Order of the Day' as follows:

'If a Box is attacked it must, I repeat *must,* hold out, reporting the attack to Group or Corps, who will send tanks which can mop up the enemy. We must keep our landing strips safe to use and our aircraft to fly. We can then beat the enemy for certain. Air Force humour will beat the Jap, who has none. Good Luck! Good Shooting!'

I spoke to the airmen in the Group saying that we were to expect to be isolated for a bit, but that I personally had no doubt whatever as to the final outcome of the whole affair, and the whole attitude and atmosphere everywhere was, in fact, great.

It was impossible to give the pilots too much flying, they were always clamouring for more, and the airmen were prepared to work all day and all night to keep the aircraft flying and to guard them, and everywhere I went it was the same story. They were all itching for the Jap to try to attack their particular spot, as they were convinced that their own defence system was the best ever and were longing to prove that they could use a rifle or machine-gun as well as the regular soldier.

Some of the isolated radar stations had very small parties,

but the same spirit prevailed as at the bigger stations, and it was refreshing and encouraging to go around. I took to sleeping in the office about this time in order to be near the Defence Officer and the War Room, and we gave up 'afternoon tea' in the mess and had a sort of high tea instead about 18.30 hrs, in order to enable officers and bearers to get to duty positions before dark.

All officers and airmen carried arms and steel helmets, and we really felt we were at war, emphasised by the noise around us of 5.5 howitzers, 25-pounders and mortars of our own, and the guns and mortars of the enemy. Corps put a battery of 25-pounders just in front of our Group H.Q. in the valley, and a battery of 5.5 howitzers just round the spur of our hill. It was the intention of the Commander Royal Artillery not to let the Jap have undisturbed sleep—and I hope they disturbed the Japs as much as they did us!

April came with the Japs getting still closer every day, and the nights getting noisier. On the 5th, the 17th Division started to get back into the valley, with General Cowan. They had had a very hard retreat down the Tiddim Road, under very bad mountain conditions, and with continual sniping, harassing attacks and road blocks by the Japs. However, they got in with practically all their transport, and brought in successfully about 1,200 wounded. These we proceeded to evacuate by air out of the valley over the next few days.

I got General Cowan to come into the mess on the 17th and give a talk to most of the pilots from the squadrons in the valley, and this went down very well as he was very appreciative of the work they had done to assist him materially in getting his division back into the valley.

Lord Louis Mountbatten, the Supreme Allied Commander, visited us next day, after which we had one or two interesting shows by watching our Vengeances and Hurribombers bombing the Jap on the hills on the other side of the valley about seven miles away. The 'Supremo' on his frequent visits was a great morale booster for the troops, airmen as well as soldiers. He gave groups informal talks, standing on an oil-drum or crate (which the officer in charge always 'just happened' to have adjacent!). He invariably was able to tell them something which had not appeared in *S.E.A.C.*—the excellent local newspaper produced by Frank Owen—and he was always confident and enthusiastic.

I started a form of mild dysentery in this period; my diary entries record: 'Early to bed in the office, but woken up by *a*) Thunder, *b*) Teleprinters, *c*) Gunfire, *d*) Air Raid and *e*) tummy three times; *a*) went by in the usual manner, *b*) a continual clacking in the basha next door to my office in the inevitable maddening way, *c*) periodical and annoying, *d*) noisy for a short time, with bombs and ack-ack guns and *e*) far the greatest nuisance of the lot.' A day or two later I was given M & B by the Doc which made me feel very bad and gave a sleepless night, but made a lightning cure so was well worth it. Throughout this period we had R.A.F. Regiment posts all round the top of the hill to prevent Jap patrols getting over and down on to H.Q. In the middle of the month one of these patrols heard an approaching body from the other side of the hill, and later saw crouching forms. Their challenge was met with silence. A little later sounds advanced up the hill, and in the light of the moon they could again see the crouching figures, and they fired. The advance converted into a retreat—by, it was then discovered, baboons!

About this time Jap air raids and thunderstorms were both fairly frequent. On the 19th I flew up to Jorhat and then on to Dinjan to contact the American General there, and back to Jorhat for the night, after dinner with XXXIII Corps and a visit to Dergaon. The following day I went to Lanka for lunch with Nos. 5 and 11 Squadrons; on to Silchar for tea and back to Imphal for supper, where I found the strip had been shelled for a short time, somewhat unsuccessfully by the Jap, just after I had left the previous day.

We had five Jap air raids between April 22nd and 25th, but not very serious and on each occasion we knocked some of their aircraft down. Rain in the last few days of the month, however, necessitated No. 607 Squadron having to leave their strip, as the bunkers and trenches were all swamped. We brought the Spitfires to Imphal with its all-weather surface, and crowded the officers and men into Group Headquarters. I had five or six living in my two rooms while I was using the office, and it soon became a lucky thing to live in these rooms as every member of the Squadron who did so got at least one Jap aircraft confirmed to his credit.

On the last day of the month Palel airstrip was attacked by Jap troops and in spite of many hours' exchange of rifle- and machine-gun fire, not a single airman fired into the black in a meaningless manner; I was very pleased with their steadfastness and discipline, and went down to see them first thing in the morning.

In the early part of May I wrote in my diary, over the space of ten days: 'Things are getting far too standard to keep a daily diary. A Jap fighter sweep, sometimes with a few bombers, and almost always we get about two destroyed, two or three probably destroyed, and several damaged, in exchange for nothing. The land battle is near, but it seems to be at its nearest—I hope!'

On the 16th I flew down via Kumbhirgram to Comilla, where I had a very good dinner, and came back the following day, again via Kumbhirgram. On the next day we got four Japs destroyed, five probably destroyed, and six damaged, for the loss of two Spitfires.

From about May 20th the weather gradually became more and more 'monsoony'; somewhat feeble Jap raids still took place in between, when we usually got a few of their aircraft. They did unfortunately jump four Hurricanes, intent on their low-flying tactical reconnaissance. On the 26th the monsoon definitely started with day and night of heavy rain. On June 6th I took my Group Intelligence Officer, Sqn. Ldr. Hargrove, round a circuit of my 'parish' after one false weather start. At Dergaon we thoroughly enjoyed playing a round of golf on the local tea planters' course. It was very hot and sticky but Hargrove and I beat the locals on their own course—out of practice as we were!

The following day we went to Jorhat, Kumbhirgram and Silchar, and flew back to Imphal in the evening of the following day, after watching rain all day long. The rain increased until the 16th when there were only six Dakotas bringing in supplies to the besieged garrison, and there were no operational sorties in the Group. Otherwise, every day Dakotas, Wellingtons and even Mitchells were pouring in a steady stream with rations, bombs, ammunition and supplies of all sorts, and the Japs who were sitting on the hills surrounding us, thinking they had us bottled up, must have been infuriated to see the besieged getting a regular supply of everything, while they, the besiegers, were short of food, ammunition, medical supplies—short of practically everything, chiefly owing to the attacks on their lines of communication by aircraft in the Group.

On the 17th Noël Coward gave us a concert in the evening, which was very good. He flew into the valley with his accompanist and piano, an electrician and batman, and guide, and spent several days going from one unit to another, coming to us for the first one. He stayed to dinner afterwards, and then, in a fit of temperamental petulance, steamed out of the mess, but apologised quite gracefully by letter the next day.

After four or five days of more heavy rain, the road was opened once more by XXXIII Corps, coming down on June 22nd, and the first convoy came in only a few hours later. In this convoy they had a psychological triumph by bringing in 75 per cent beer. This ration enabled every officer and man—Army and R.A.F.—in the valley to have a bottle of beer, and this did more than most things could to prove that we were indeed relieved, and that things other than necessities could come in from out of the valley. We had endured three or four months without such luxuries as a beer ration, and had lived mostly on bully beef, baked beans and soya link sausages, all on a slightly reduced scale, although I think very few people were hungry or complained very much about the amount, only the deadly monotony of it.

From this date on the whole state of the campaign improved daily. XXXIII Corps joined us in the valley and five Brigades started out to capture Ukhrul, and the Jap was being pushed back on all sides of the valley. After a fortnight's steady improvement in the state of the war, I flew to Delhi for a conference, starting on the 7th July, in a Harvard, and after about nine hours' flying got there for lunch, on the 8th. I spent the rest of the day and most of the next with the Goddards, and attended a conference of A.O.C.s on the morning and afternoon of the 10th, going to the broadcasting station in between to give a broadcast on life at Imphal during the siege. That night there was a party at the senior officers' mess at which were present 27 air officers.

After another two days of more or less solid flying I got back to Imphal on the 12th. Until the end of that month and well into August, there was a steady daily improvement, with the Japs retreating as hard as they could go, while our aircraft spent their time chasing them, shooting up road transport and river craft, and on August 5th we recaptured Tamu with its valuable strip, the loss of which we had felt for months. Here the Jap had very serious losses, and hundreds of corpses were found all around the area of the strip; most of the Japs died from starvation and disease, due again, largely, to the Group's attacks on the lines of communication.

About this time a new invasion started in Imphal; this time visitors. All ranks of every Service descended on us to see where the war had been. Steve (Air Vice-Marshal C. A. Stevens) had come out to join the 3rd Tactical Air Force as Air Officer Administration and came up for two or three days to see round the area. The Viceroy for two days with inspections of units, the Allied C.-in-C., Air Vice-Marshals Gibbs and Whitworth-Jones and many more visitors at lower levels. Most were welcome, but not all.

On August 16th my S.A.S.O.—Warrington—left to command No. 177 Wing. He was relieved by Athol Forbes from No. 165 Wing, who had been with me at Northolt in 1940 as a Flight Commander in No. 303 (Polish) Squadron. Air Marshal Alec Coryton took over 3rd Tactical Air Force from Jack Baldwin, and came up to see us on the 18th.

Towards the end of August I decided to take four days' leave and tried to get to Calcutta on the 25th, but after groping my way through rain for a long time, had to turn back from the Dacca area and spend the night at Agatarla, but managed to make it the following morning after much more rain. I stayed with Air Commodore 'Tog' Mellersh of No. 231 Group and managed to do some odd bits of necessary shopping, and had some very good meals both in Mellersh's mess and at the Bengal Club. I had several enjoyable bathes in the local swimming pool: a good full-length bath adjoined my bedroom. I managed to get several letters written and had quite a good break.

On the way back I was summoned to Comilla where I got wrapped up into 'plans' and had to go back past Calcutta to Ranchi, where I spent four or five days planning forthcoming operations with IV Corps. This was in a way satisfactory, as I was planning forward moves, but it was pretty obvious from the start that that particular operation would not be necessary, as was subsequently proved.

Until the end of August we had a great deal more rain, and operations were seriously curtailed thereby, but we did a fair amount more planning, this time with XXXIII Corps, and the future started to take on a rosier prospect. In order to prepare for personal moves into jungly locations, I started about this time to make a caravan for myself, consisting of an office trailer taken off its chassis and put on to one of a four-wheel drive 3-ton Thornycroft lorry. This was designed after much thought and care, and a team of enthusiasts from various units started in to build it under the supervision of my Group M.T. Officer, Flt. Lt. Adams. The whole of October was taken up almost entirely with visitors, visitors and more visitors, but I heard on the 28th that I was promoted to Air Vice-Marshal as from the 18th.

In the first week of November the visitors still continued: the Allied Air C.-in-C., the Air Commander, General McConnel, Air Vice-Marshal Harcourt-Smith, Air Commodore Brook, Sir Ronald Cross (High Commissioner for Australia) and the Nawab of Bhopal were among the most notable.

I had to go to Calcutta twice during the month for conferences and found myself getting quite a twin-engined pilot, having taken a Beechcraft Expediter, which had a fair cruising speed and takes a reasonable load of passengers and goods with comfort.

In the middle of December there was a big party at Army Headquarters (14th Army having moved up to the valley into XXXIII Corps late Headquarters, after the Corps had moved well forward. This followed the dubbing of Generals Slim, Scoones, Christison and Stopford with their knighthoods for the victory of the Imphal campaign, and was carried out by the Viceroy. General Slim, the Army Commander, was incensed that the Army should have got four knighthoods and the R.A.F. represented by No. 221 Group got not even a Mention in Dispatches! There were present at the ceremony, Lady Wavell and Felicity, Lord Louis Mountbatten the Supremo, the Allied Air C.-in-C., General Leese the new C.-in-C. Allied Land Forces S.E. Asia, wives and families of the new knights, and many other high-ranking but not quite so exalted personages.

This all meant quite a big responsibility for me as this tempting array was spread out in front of a big parade of troops and guards of honour within range of Jap aircraft. However, the Jap apparently knew nothing about it, or were scared of the patrol we had flying overhead; anyway, we were not disturbed. Some time later I was given the C.B. for the Group's work at Imphal, after General Slim had personally complained to Air Ministry.

I had another conference at Calcutta with General Stratemeyer of Eastern Command, who were now our superiors since 3rd T.A.F. had been absorbed by them. It was a nuisance having to fly 400 miles there and back for conferences. On the 21st I flew down to see the new strips we were starting to occupy in our advance after the Japs.

After this trip I told them back at Headquarters that while flying over a Jap-held strip in my Hurricane, I had seen a Jap two-seater bomber, got it well in my sights and pressed the firing button and that I had left it crashed into the trees at the side of the strip. All of this was strictly true but—a big but—when I first saw it it was already crashed into the side of the strip. I thought I'd put some more holes in it to prevent it being repaired, only to find that when I pressed the trigger button, my guns did not fire. The armourer had not connected it up, and there I was, over enemy territory unable to defend myself or to do any damage. I flew back as fast as I could in order to have words with that man.

The whole Group including H.Q. was now busy moving or preparing to move forward. The Headquarters, joined with Fourteenth Army, became a combined Headquarters. We managed to get a very good Christmas Day in at all the units I was able to visit, finishing up with an excellent dinner ourselves. On Boxing Day and the 27th the Group H.Q. gave a most entertaining pantomime at which I sang some of my foolishly worded songs of the earlier part of the war—as a surprise guest artist.

I saw the New Year in in an interesting and unusual manner. I went with Mills, my A.O.A., and two ENSA artistes (my partner being a sweet young thing of fifty-five) to Group Captain Chacksfield's No. 910 Wing at Wangjang. Here he had organised an open-air party for the pilots and airmen, including the roasting of a whole ox. This was duly done throughout the day on a spit over a large wood fire. On each side of the ox were arranged counters with little 'V' roofs over them on which were served the extra Christmas ration of beer and also a rum punch. On the other side on a similar counter was a vast number of loaves of bread being cut up to receive slices of ox.

At approximately quarter to twelve, Chacksfield, who is well over six feet, wearing an enormous chef's cap which made him well over seven, seized a huge carving knife and fork and proceeded to cut the first ceremonial slice, which he handed to me in the fingers, and which I proceeded to eat midst deafening cheers from all round. Our lady visitors (the only two there) and the A.O.A. were the next to get their share. After this we were given a tin mug each with a dollop of rum punch to drink to everybody's good health and good wishes for the New Year. Rockets and Very lights were fired to signal in the New Year, after which in an air of good wishes, grasping hands from all ranks and a general demonstration of grand morale, we left, going first with Chacksfield on to the strip, where we were shown all the Thunderbolts lined up in the moonlight, all with their bombs on ready for the show in a few hours' time—they had carried out one particularly successful attack the previous afternoon.

The visitors were very impressed with the long, silent lines of aircraft, with their obvious potential threat to the Jap, their 500 lb bombs hanging on each side, and very sober airmen on guard between every few aircraft, as they were such a contrast to the cheering, singing crowd we had just left. The younger lady visitor asked for a bit of chalk and wrote a suitable rude message on one of the bombs, feeling that she was doing her bit against the Jap. The older one told me that she had never missed seeing in the New Year as long as she could remember, but never had she seen one in in such an impressive and dramatic manner . . . and she was a Scot.

We then drove back the fifteen or twenty miles to Imphal, deposited them at the ENSA bungalow, and went back to bed. So ended the story of 1944.

19

Victory

The year 1945 started in a fever of plans and preparations for movement, packing up our old Headquarters at Imphal and closing down my nice bungalow. My caravan was packed and loaded and sent on its way and on January 3rd I flew in my Harvard with Shaw, my personal assistant, to Kalemyo, where the new combined Fourteenth Army/221 Group Headquarters was to be; it was at the lower end of the Kabaw Valley, approximately 100 miles south and a bit east of Imphal.

The Kabaw Valley was known as the 'Valley of Death' because of a reputation for malaria and typhus, but we did not, however, intend remaining there until the unhealthy time of the year started. In point of fact, during the five weeks we were there, there was very little sickness indeed, also everyone took mepacrine tablets daily.

We had various strips up and down the valley, mostly new ones made by us such as Yasagyo, Indaingalle, Kalemyo and Thazi, and also Taukyan which the Jap had conveniently made for us. After our experiences of the previous year when we were pushed back and subsequently surrounded and besieged for three months, this forward move was a great relief and everyone was full of confidence.

Headquarters was sited in an area from which elephant grass had been cut and removed. This grass is very dense and grows anything from six to twenty feet or more in height. It gets almost like a small bamboo and is impossible to penetrate without a heavy, sharp knife to cut a way through, and I shudder to think what might have happened to some of my fellows who had to come down in their aircraft or parachutes and land into the middle of an area of this stuff. The camp was, of course, all canvas and caravans, and my caravan justified the trouble and time that had been put into it. It was very comfortable and quite efficient as an office as well.

Now that we were living within a few yards of each other and fed in the same mess, I got to know General Slim, the Army Commander, better all the time. He was a grand fellow and one who fully appreciated and realised what the Group was doing for the Army, and that without it they could not have advanced a yard, indeed they might well have gone in the other direction!

We were busy moving our Wings all this time, keeping them close behind the advancing Corps—IV and XXXIII—and from first to last there were no less than 128 squadron moves with scarcely interrupting a single sortie. In fact for the month there was 6,349 sorties and over 1,000 tons of bombs dropped. The task facing my group was as follows:

1. Destruction of the Japanese Air Force in Burma whenever possible in order to maintain air superiority, and to ensure protection against the enemy for air transport aircraft engaged in essential supply operations.
2. Provision of adequate direct support for the ground forces by Hurricane and Thunderbolt fighter-bombers assisted, if necessary, by Liberator or Mitchell aircraft from other Groups.
3. Destruction of enemy defences in advance of the Allied ground forces with assistance, if necessary, from heavy and medium bombers, including the Mosquito and Beaufighter squadrons of the Group.
4. Isolation of the main enemy forces by disrupting lines of communication by day and night; destruction of the enemy's installations and supplies both in the immediate battle area and on his lines of communication, and repeated bombing of Japanese Headquarters to engender confusion.

The strength of the Group grew and at this time we had Nos. 5, 11, 20, 34, 42, 60 and 113 Squadrons of Hurricanes for close support, supplemented by Nos. 79, 146 and 261 Squadrons of Thunderbolt long-range fighter-bombers. There were also No. 28 and No. 1 (R.I.A.F.) Squadrons of Hurricanes for fighter reconnaissance work, and Nos. 45, 47 and 82 of Mosquito and Beaufighter fighter-bombers in the long-range tactical role. For our defence we had Nos. 17, 152, 155 and 607 Squadrons of Spitfires and a detachment of No. 89 Squadron's night-fighting Beaufighters. Additionally, I had a detachment of No. 681 Squadron photo reconnaissance Spitfires, and the Group's communication squadron which provided, among other things, the aircraft for my own visits.

In the early days of the advance there was a big attack on Gangaw further down another valley. Just alongside this village a light aircraft strip had been made of about 400 yards and the Army Commander and Brigadier Lethbridge, with Air Marshal Coryton who was visiting me, were keen to see this attack by air and ground forces of IV Corps. We flew down in five Stinson L-5s from Kalemyo to Gangaw. I had not been there before and was leading the five aircraft and asked Air Marshal Coryton, my passenger, who had the only map, to do the navigating. Unfortunately he did not spot the place and we flew on with our distinguished passengers over enemy-occupied territory. I got more and more suspicious of the countryside below, and decided to turn back after some twenty miles and fortunately found the strip myself.

We saw quite an impressive attack by the B-25 Mitchells of the American 12th Bombardment Group under Colonel Dalton and our own Thunderbolts and Hurricanes, after which our troops went in.

During the month I went several times to our various strips in the forward area, some of which had been bombed by the Jap on several occasions and one had been attacked by a 'jitter' party with grenades and rifles on the ground.

On February 9th we moved our Combined Headquarters another 100 miles on, this time to Monywa where we made ourselves a remarkably good office and domestic area. Monywa was a town on the River Chindwin, a big river—and had obviously, before the war, been a remarkably pleasant place, buildings being of good-looking brick with impressive pagodas and temples, well laid out, plenty of beautiful trees and all facing on the river frontage.

Alas for the ravages of war, as first the Jap bombed it in 1942 and then we bombed it after the Jap had captured it in the same year. Then we bombed it again good and hearty in 1945 to boost him out of it again. The result was that it became one of the worst blitzed towns that I have seen, there being not one single building undamaged and the vast majority completely demolished.

We made our Headquarters offices at the north, least damaged, end of the town and General Slim, his Brigadier General Staff Lethbridge, 'Tiny' Vasse (my S.A.S.O.) and I, Army War Room and our Intelligence, all worked in what had been the Law Courts. Other buildings close by held our own War Room, Fighter Ops Room, Signals, Admin Staff and the Army 'G' and 'Q' staffs, signals and other arms. There were something like a dozen combined officers' messes shared by Army and R.A.F. of approximately the same ranks and as much as possible of the same type of job: 'A' Mess, the senior one in which the R.A.F. was represented by 'Tiny' Vasse, Mills, the Air Officer Admin, and myself, was a roofless and frontless house facing the river on which we had put a tarpaulin as a roof for the downstairs portion, the only part used. The other members of 'A' Mess were General Slim, of course, with Brigadiers Lethbridge, Alf Snelling, 'Welsher' Welshman, Bill Bowen and Hasted.

My caravan, Vasse's, Mills' and visitors' tents were some 50 yards from the mess, overlooking the river, and undoubtedly the best site in the whole camp. The temperature began to go up steadily almost from the day of arrival and the river proved a real godsend to bathe in during the evening to get clean and cool. In the middle of February the temperature was round about the 91 or 92 degrees Fahrenheit, and this crept up steadily until the first half of April when it was about 108 in the shade, and pretty sticky at the same time. Everybody spent

most of their day stripped to the waist, with the exception of mealtimes. Sleeping outside at night under a mosquito net in the same manner was the best arrangement for possible comfort.

One incident I remember at this time—the C.O. of one of the Mosquito squadrons, Wing Commander R. J. Walker, found a good target about 200 miles into enemy territory and dived down with a gun attack. The enemy, firing at him, hit his windscreen, pieces of which flew up into his face and eyes, as he had foolishly pushed his goggles up on to the top of the head for better vision. Immediately blinded, he automatically pulled out of the dive and into a climb, whereupon his navigator (beside him in a Mosquito), realising what had happened, told Walker what to do—to push the stick forward or back and so on, and then to work the rudder bar so as to get the aeroplane back on course for friendly country.

They successfully covered two hundred miles, by which time Walker could see a little out of one eye, and attempted a landing on the Monywa strip, commanded by Group Captain Finlay, the one-time famous Olympic hurdler. Walker's judgement was, of course, seriously affected and he was nowhere near on his first attempt, so put on his engines to go round again for a second.

The Group Captain thought, 'What is this fool trying to do? He's behaving like a first soloist.' But after the second failure to get on to the runway, he realised that this was no fool, but someone in serious trouble, and got into his jeep and went to the far end of the runway where he considered he would probably be needed. Walker, keeping calm-headed, tried a third time when a blur of runway appeared and did, in fact, put his aeroplane down successfully on to the ground, but too fast, so it overran and tipped up on its nose quite gently at the end. I happened to be visiting the sick and wounded in our 100-bed No. 60 Mobile Field Hospital R.A.F. when Walker was brought in. When told I was there, his one thought and request was that he would not lose his squadron. I could only tell him that I was sure the surgeons would be able to save his eyes, and if so, of course, he would stay. I was able to say 'good show' before he went into a spotless operating theatre, made in one of the hundreds of pagodas—Buddhist temples—a small porch of which had been scrubbed and whitewashed and a good light added for the job.

This hospital had just previously been swamped by an early monsoon downpour and was flooded several inches deep—in fact almost up to the springs of the beds—in the tents. The wonderful nurses had carried on from ward to ward until they were soaked, when they retired to their tents and put on bathing costumes in which they continued to work on the patients. There was only one seriously ill at the time, and one of the nurses sat by his bed, holding an umbrella over him, and did save his life.

While thanking them and congratulating them on their fortitude and good humour, the surgeon got busy on Wing Commander Walker's eyes. He was able to extract many pieces of glass from both eyes; one eye became quite fit, but the other has never been 100 per cent since, and I am sorry to say he did have to leave his squadron and return home. Both he and his navigator were, very deservedly, decorated for a fine, level-headed and calm performance.

Most of the flying was carried out over enemy-held territory, of course, and on many occasions aircraft were shot down by ground fire, as much of this flying had to be at very low altitude, attacking transport of all kinds—motor vehicles, carts, river boats and even elephants. When possible, pilots would climb away before an engine seized up and jump out in a parachute; many, alas, were never heard of again, either having fallen into enemy hands, died of wounds, or been unable to escape from the jungle.

A few managed to get back, but very few. One had been seen to come down not very far from our forward position and word was sent to the infantry to look for him, if possible. After two days of hacking his way through tall elephant grass, he saw what he thought was a Japanese patrol and turned back and ran into thicker jungle to hide. The patrol was, in fact, of Gurkhas who were searching for him. On seeing him run, taking him for a Jap, they opened fire and killed him. A tragic finish for a brave young man who had beaten the jungle and was almost home.

Another pilot successfully brought off an absolute copybook escape. He had with him his emergency escape kit which included limited food, medical supplies, water and a compass. He started walking, steering by compass, but after two days during which time he had not come upon any water, he realised that he was sweating away his valuable liquid, so lay up in the shade by day and moved by night. He was lucky as there was very good moonlight for most of his time, but he gradually finished all the water and he was getting very desperate after three very dry days. When almost delirious, he came across a muddy patch of ground into which he flung himself and sucked the mud.

After a time he realised what he was doing and that he must be near a stream, which he found and filled his water-bottle, into which he put six water-purifying tablets instead of the usual one, thinking this would catch up, as it were, the dirty water he had already taken in. Apparently it did do just that, as he suffered no ill effects and was able to continue his walk. He had by then finished the items of food such as compressed chocolate and continued entirely on Horlicks malted milk tablets which he rationed himself to six a day.

He was able to keep by the stream for quite a long time as it was running on the course he was walking. By wading he missed much jungle and made reasonable progress. He walked all night and slept and rested by day, when, after sleeping, he got the needle and thread from the jungle kit and mended the tears in his shirt and trousers, sewed on the torn-off buttons and darned his socks. He washed himself and all his clothing and dried it in the sun, and, by thus keeping busy, maintained sanity and hope.

When he was almost back he found a path which he followed and, on rounding a bend, almost ran into a Jap. He turned back and ran out of sight and jumped behind a thick bush alongside the path. The Japanese sentry ran round after him and stopped right alongside the bush, whereupon the pilot jumped out on to him and brought him crashing to the ground.

As he fell with the Jap, the pilot automatically put out his hand which happened to fall on a stone about the size of a cricket-ball, which he picked up and bashed down on to the skull of the Jap. He heard an ominous crack and the figure went inert, so he jumped up and ran clear—being very careful at every bend. He saw the rest of the patrol sleeping, unaware of what had happened to their sentry. He was, also, fired at by the first Indian soldier he met, but fortunately was not hit and managed to make himself recognised and, finally, welcomed. After twenty-one days of strenuous walking, wading and jungle hacking, he was brought into our H.Q. fit and strong, and a jolly good advertisement for Horlicks! I gave him a bath in my famous full-length bath, a bottle of beer and a change of clothing, followed by a good meal. His only request immediately, was for permission to keep his beard, which was quite handsome after three weeks, until he reported back to his squadron, as he wanted to show it off to his friends!

When we were at Monywa the Permanent Under Secretary of State came to visit. He had never been out East at all and was a bit 'mazed' after a quick transition from his office in only two or three days by air, to jungly war!

We were just having our evening bathes in the River Chindwin when a dust-storm—a rare occurrence—blew up. We dived for our caravans and tents till it swirled past in thick, choking dust, and then a bathe was doubly welcome, but my poor Air Officer Administration, Air Commodore Mills, pulled on his bathing-trunks which had been hanging up in his tent, and gave a yell of pain having been stung by a scorpion in a very tender exclusively male portion of his anatomy! He had a field-telephone in his tent, fortunately, and was able to grasp it and gasp out, 'Get a doctor immediately!' Owing to the general din of the storm, none of us nearby heard him, but the doctor did get to him and 'froze' him, after which he slowly recovered, but only after considerable pain.

After our bathe we sat on the bund overlooking the river with a bottle of gin, kept for visitors' occasions. While drinking this, movement was seen in the grass just in front of us, and one of us luckily had a stout stick with which he bashed and duly killed a krait, a particularly venomous snake.

In the middle of the night following, I woke in my bed outside my caravan and saw, silhouetted on the river bund, a small puma, walking sedately along some twenty feet away. I reached out of my mosquito net to get my rifle, which I always kept handy, but it heard my movement and shot up a tree, on the reverse side of the trunk. I could see his head peeping round, looking at me. He was a handsome animal, dark coloured with a particularly long tail, sticking almost straight out behind as he walked. After a time I decided he meant me no harm, so, with rifle inside the netting, I went back to sleep.

When our very senior civil servant visitor was called by my good Corporal Clayton, driver-cum-batman, he shot out of the netting as Clayton was lifting up the other side to give him a cup of tea! He was convinced that, apart altogether from Japanese, Burma was no place for him!

The snake episode reminds me of a nice little couplet which appeared in our service paper *S.E.A.C.*:

> 'The Krait very seldom has one over the eight:
> And the Cobra is even sobra.'

During March the battle of Central Burma waxed and waxed until the Jap burst and the battle was very definitely won. The Group beat all previous records with 8,745 sorties flown and an estimated 98 buildings, 445 bashas, 14 bridges, 143 vehicles and a locomotive and items of rolling stock destroyed. I felt I had kept my promise to the Army Commander that we would exceed the maximum rates for some time until the battle was won, on condition I could knock it down immediately afterwards.

A secret document of the Air Ministry laid down three degrees of operational intensity in which the number of hours were to be flown daily by aircraft, normal, extra and intensive. (The last was not to be exceeded for more than a day or two.) These figures were to assist the Org Staff in the requirements for petrol and oil, and the depots for replacement aircraft and engines. Almost every aeroplane of the twenty-one squadrons in the Group exceeded the maximum possible—not for a 'day or two' but for *six consecutive months*. It was a wonderful effort of the pilots and the ground crews and also of the Aircraft Depots back in India which kept us supplied throughout with remarkably little waiting, though they were several hundred miles away.

On March 20th Mandalay fell and on the 21st I flew General Slim in an L-5 and landed him on the racecourse there, after which we did a triumphal entry into the town. About a mile of the road inside Fort Dufferin was lined by troops of the 19th Division who had captured Mandalay, and General Rees, its Commander, drove the first jeep with the Army Commander beside him and myself in the back, through the town and fort. We were followed by other jeeps with General Stopford, Commander XXXIII Corps and Generals Gracey and Nicholson commanding the 20th and 2nd Divisions. General Slim hauled up the Union Jack on a raised platform, gave three cheers for the King Emperor and made a short speech into the microphone for subsequent broadcast by the B.B.C.

Driving out of the Fort again was impressive as all the troops cheered as the General drove by, and they looked fit and happy to have done what they had done and their morale appeared grand, British, Indian and Gurkha alike.

On the way back we landed at another forward strip and went up to the front line in the 2nd Division area, and the General spoke to several groups of men, each time introducing me as the owner of all the aircraft without which none of them would have been where they were! A most interesting day, though we heard that the following day two officers had been blown up and killed by a mine in the road over which the General and I had passed twice!

On April 2nd, my A.O.A., Air Commodore Mills and I flew up in two L-5s to Maymyo, where we landed on the race-course in order to connect with the Chief Engineer Fourteenth Army, Brigadier Hasted, and the Chief Signals Officer, Brigadier Bowen, to inspect the old Jap strip at Anasakan.

Maymyo must have been a very beautiful place in peacetime.

It is a little over 3,000 feet high and the climate was wonderful compared with Monywa. The buildings in the town were good, plenty of space around each with what must have been beautiful gardens, though now terribly overgrown. Hedges which had been clipped at about 4–5 feet high were growing another 8 or 10 feet. Everything had therefore coarsened, the grass wanted cutting and the flower-beds remaking. The lake still bore evidence of lovely gardens round, with varieties of flowering trees and shrubs. The club had been burnt to the ground by the Jap, but one could see what a beautiful situation it must have had, looking out on to a fine green golf course of which the bunkers could still be seen.

While we were there we went to the building used by the Kempetai, the Jap organisation equivalent to the Gestapo. Here we saw the cells where the prisoners and suspected locals were put and tortured. One small cell, measuring 10 by 8 feet was used for 25 people. They were never allowed out and were kept in there for anything up to six months. Because of the crowd it was impossible for anyone to lie down. The sanitary conditions defy consideration.

Just prior to this time the Army made its spectacular and now famous thrust across country to Meiktila, some 80 miles south of Mandalay, cutting the Jap lines of communication to the north and north-west, catching him completely by surprise and causing tremendous casualties.

It was considered essential to make the river crossing a surprise in order to carry out the dash across country to Meiktila. In order to achieve this and to keep the enemy guessing where a crossing would be made, many ruses were employed, such as concentrations of vehicles to mislead in the direction of thrusts and wireless traffic emanating from fictitious Headquarters and formations. Ingenious packets made by firework factories were dropped by aircraft in the river at night which floated downstream and, after a lapse of time, simulated battle noises to give a false impression of troop positions.

After initial confusion, the Jap reacted strongly to the main thrust and concentrated counter-attacks against the airstrip where air supplies were being flown in as soon as that was put in order. It must be appreciated that every member of the Fourteenth Army and No. 221 Group was, during this whole period of many months, being supplied entirely by air with rations, ammunition, shells, bombs, petrol, etc. The R.A.F. representatives at Meiktila put up a first-class show at this critical stage.

The R.A.F. Regiment proved themselves grand fighters, and so did the Servicing Commandos, radar personnel and the Air Formation Signals. Those, mostly the R.A.F. Regiment, of course, held a 'Box' on the edge of the strip, and the local Army troops withdrew every night into another 'Box' further behind, and left the strip open for recapture every night by the enemy, and our lads were, therefore, in the front position. During this time they had a considerable amount of fighting and inflicted very many casualties on the enemy, but of course, unfortunately, lost several killed and wounded themselves, including their C.O., a first-class Wing Commander by name of Lander.

Eventually the area was cleared, other columns came across country to strengthen the garrison, and we were able to operate from the strip with very little interference. I took my P.A.—Shaw—there for the first time on the 5th April to have a look at the place and to visit General Messervy, the IV Corps Commander. The rest of the month I spent in the usual way, in the office and visiting the Wings at such places as Thedaw, Kinmagan, Myingyan and Magwe.

On the 26th April we moved the Combined Army/Group Headquarters to Meiktila, and after one night in a house our caravans joined us, and we made a small compound for Vasse, Mills and myself on the edge of a most attractive lake, the saving grace of the place.

Meiktila again must have been a very pleasant place in peacetime, with good buildings, a reasonable number of trees, some of them of the most beautiful flowering varieties with attractive scents, but the main part of the town was laid flat by us with bombs and shells, mostly during the recent battles. However, a few quite good houses were left on the outskirts, and in these we made our offices and messes, and lived in our caravans and under canvas. The climate was pleasanter than at Monywa, being appreciably cooler due to the breeze which blew across the lake. Bathing was very pleasant and we used to get into the lake most mornings and evenings.

About this time the monsoon preliminaries came and we had frequent heavy storms, gales, thunder and lightning and heavy rain. This would render airstrips unserviceable and destroy or damage aircraft by tearing some away from their picketing, giving me grey hairs with worry as to whether or not the engineers were going to be able to make the rolled mud airstrips for all-weather use, usable throughout the monsoon, in time, by using rolls of bithess.*

At this time the American B-25 Group, still under Colonel Dalton, carried out much invaluable work when our aircraft could not operate because of the wet unusable runways. They flew in from the Arakan—with their greater fuel endurance—and carried out close support duties with the advancing ground troops, being called in on to pockets of resistance and attacking them with bombs and gunfire. This they did with conspicuous success and filled a gap that could not have been done in any other way. I was able to get the Colonel awarded a D.F.C. for the splendid work carried out by himself and his squadrons.

While at Meiktila the end of the war in Europe occurred—V.E. Day. We listened on our wireless to the rejoicings at home, to Big Ben, the Prime Minister's voice . . . and felt a bit hard done by, having to go on fighting and in the monsoon, for goodness only knew how much longer.

Early in May after much planning and argument the rush down to Rangoon was successfully accomplished, and a quite unnecessary sea assault made with parachute landings and all the paraphernalia of war to capture a town already evacuated by the enemy!

This rush down the 300 miles from Meiktila along the railway on the east and the Irrawaddy river further west, cut off many thousands of Japs from their supplies and Headquarters, and organised resistance ceased.

The capture of Rangoon was made by Wing Commander Saunders and Flight Lieutenant Stephen of No. 110 Squadron

* Bituminised hessian.

in a Mosquito. They flew over the town on a reconnaissance and saw, first, the prison with large letters on the roof—'Japs Gone, Extract Digit'. This wording could only have been made by British prisoners. They then went to the Rangoon aerodrome at Mingaladon seeing white sheets being waved, landed and got hold of a car and drove into the empty town and to the prison where they were able to tell the enthusiastic audience that they would soon be freed.

However, there were still all those little perishers to mop up as, unlike most other nations of the world, they rarely gave themselves up, but fought to the last round of the last man. Both the Army and ourselves were constantly searching out and destroying comparatively small parties who still continued to attempt to escape, crossing our positions at night in order to rejoin their own forces.

In the middle of May we were going through worrying times trying to get Headquarters fixed in Rangoon, and Service squabbles were non-stop because the local army troops would steal the buildings allocated to Group units, our hospitals or depots.

We soon got a Wing into nearby Mingaladon with a control organisation to protect ourselves and the docks which were able to take in three medium-sized ships at a time in a fortnight or so and could unload about 1,000 tons a day, although the Jap had demolished most of the docks that we had not previously blown up by air attack.

In the latter half of May we sent one complete Wing Headquarters with its squadrons out of Burma back into India, because of the monsoon and the airfields were only fair-weather ones of limited use. Consequently I had several farewells to make; a series at Maida Vale, the name of one of the strips at Magwe on the Irrawaddy, and at Thedaw near Meiktila.

Towards the end of May my 'innards', conforming to nearly everyone else's, started to go phoney, and a lot of us felt very cheap and looked forward to the move to Rangoon as we thought the civilised change would do us good, though we knew it would be hotter and that it was a place infamous for prickly heat. The probable cause of our stomach trouble at Meiktila was that we were drinking and bathing in the water from the lake in which there was a considerable number of dead Japs, left over from the battle.

With a little preventive assistance from the doctor, I flew down to Mingaladon, Rangoon, on the 29th, and having spent one night in my new room, I was then moved to the local hospital with amoebic dysentery! This occurred the day after I received a letter from Coryton saying that I was being sent home as a reward for a successful campaign, and that Air Ministry had promised a 'good job' at home. As I felt pretty cheap, I asked to be sent home by sea, in order to have the benefit of rest and sea air and arrive home fit. Also, to be able to have all my kit with me.

The first day my temperature was taken in hospital it was just under 103, with which I had probably been walking about for some time; but with up-to-date treatment of a new type of pill and injections in various parts of my anatomy, it came down with a run and I started to pick up rapidly, sleeping a good deal of the time.

The unfortunate timing of this was that my ship left Rangoon at the same time as the triumphal parade was held, and I was thus unable to occupy my seat beside General Slim on the dais. Instead of which I crept out feeling rather sick and lonely.

Before I left I sent in a list to the Air C.-in-C. of those I especially recommended for *immediate* decorations to signify the Group's vital part in the victory. It was not until some time later that I learned these had actually been returned by Sir Keith Park, with the exception of two only—C.B.E.s for Vasse and Mills, my S.A.S.O. and A.O.A. The Group Captains commanding Wings, several Squadron Leaders and Senior N.C.O.s were cruelly ignored. I was disgusted. The Army and Corps and one or two Divisional Commanders received immediate knighthoods; No. 221 Group was not even given a Mention in Dispatches! I was, and am, ashamed of my own Service for their lack of appreciation of the share 15,000 men in twenty-one squadrons and all their necessary supporting units had taken in winning a really difficult war against a particularly determined enemy, flying over terrible country, often through unbelievable weather conditions. These conditions made servicing and repair work often more than extremely difficult . . . all on short rations (even beer ration down to three bottles per month) for a long period of time.

In no campaign was there better affiliation and co-operation between the Services and, as General Slim so frequently said, it was not only a Fourteenth Army victory but a 50/50 success with the R.A.F.

It was a saying at the time that the Fourteenth was a forgotten Army, but they must at least have *been* known in order to be forgotten, whereas No. 221 Group had never been heard of!

In General Slim's book *Defeat into Victory* he says:

'Vincent and his men piled up our debt to them until we could never repay it, and No. 221 Group R.A.F. had as big a share in our victory, when it came, as any army formation. We were proud to serve with them, but I could not help thinking that sometimes the Army recognised their achievements more readily than some of the higher Air Force Headquarters.'

Sir Keith Park sent the following signal to me on the troopship *Dunera* after I left Rangoon: 'From Allied Air Commander-in-Chief. Very sorry you unable to take your place on dais of Supreme Allied Commander at Rangoon Victory Parade today to celebrate victorious Burma Campaign which your personal efforts and great achievements of No. 221 Group under your command and in perfect partnership with the Fourteenth Army did so much to ensure. Bouchier and Vasse representing you and No. 221 Group. Park. June 15th.'

This was the only appreciative comment or action by anyone in my Service for this victory.

20

'The landing'

There's always something a little sad about coming to any kind of ending—of a chapter, a book, a career; but very often an end can be a beginning, and apart from all else there is great joy in a home-coming. Mine was almost amusing since my wife met me, metaphorically clutching a stretcher under her arm and surprised—and even, I think, a little disappointed—at finding me quite fit and brown from lying in the sun on the deck.

It was as well that I was not the poor creature she had expected, for I had not quite finished yet. Long before my leave was up—as always seemed to be the case with me—I was off once more in mid-1945 to Fighter Command Headquarters, this time as Senior Air Staff Officer to my old friend Air Marshal Sir James Robb, who had been my C.O. in No. 30 Squadron in Iraq, twenty-one years previously.

For one who enjoyed his flying, Jimmy Robb was a bad master to serve under! He also was fond of getting into the air as often as he could, so whenever I asked him if he minded if I flew up to some station to sort out a problem, he would apologise and tell me he wanted me to hold the fort as he was flying somewhere—and away he would go in his Spitfire or, later, a Meteor!

When there was a thick fog or the rain or snow was particularly heavy, he would perhaps say, 'I shall be in the office all tomorrow, so if you would like to fly off anywhere, now's your chance'! However, I did manage to get a certain amount of flying—occasionally we went together in a couple of Spitfires, which was enjoyable. I see in my log-book the usual mixture of types of aircraft flown: Proctor, Messenger, Fieseler Storch, Auster, B-25, Domine, Spitfire, Harvard, Meteor and Anson.

My first flight in a jet—a Meteor—was at Bovingdon early in 1947 and I had to land dead into a very glaring setting sun, so much so that I could not see anything looking into it. This made me approach the aerodrome from quite the wrong angle for the runway and I had to open up the engines and go round again. On the second approach Flying Control told me to go round yet again as there was 'an obstruction on the runway' so on I motored once more, seeing a Proctor just taxiing off the runway as I flew past. Third time was lucky and I duly found an empty runway, to find on reaching the hangar, that the 'obstruction' had been my Flying Officer son, Anthony, who was one of the Communication Squadron pilots there!

I made three interesting visits to see our squadrons in Germany where I saw for the first time the damage to the Ruhr and the miracle of the Cathedral at Cologne—so like that of St. Paul's in London, where devastation was all round but the beautiful building stood out stark on its own and looking, from the air, undamaged.

I sat in the S.A.S.O.'s chair for three years, longer than any predecessor, partly due to a change of command from Robb to Bill Elliot, who had not had much experience of Fighter Command previously, and I was supposed to show him the ropes. We got on well, although he called me his 'official opposition' in conferences!

Both the Nos. 11 and 12 Group Commander posts became vacant simultaneously, and I was given the honour of choosing which one to take over. Naturally I chose No. 11 Group in which I had served in the Battle of Britain and which, for its principal part in that battle, was the most famous. I had only a few miles to move from my house in Ruislip to the A.O.C.'s Residence at Hillingdon, part of Uxbridge camp.

Here I flew mostly the grand old Anson, in order to take members of the Group staff with me to various stations, also, on a few occasions, the even older De Havilland Domine biplane! The Harvard allowed me to take one other; P.A.s, two in succession, were banished to a back seat on every occasion, to their disgust, as I always preferred to fly myself. The Devon, more modern, was used on some occasions and was pleasant to fly.

Messrs Hawkers were near Uxbridge at Langley; I went to lunch with them one day, and after one or two of their gins, I asked Sydney Camm if they had an old Hurricane they could give me for old times' sake. He said they might be able to collect pieces from here and there and put one together for me, being quite keen on the idea! This, in fact, he proceeded to do, and with bits from their factories, an engine from—I believe—Halton, a propeller from somewhere else, a complete Hurricane grew, and was given the serial number LF363 and a log-book.

I went over to do the testing of it as there was no one else to do so. It was fine and after some early misfortunes, it was eventually cleared of unnecessary gun gear, etc., and with an A.O.C.'s flag painted on the side, I took it over and used it around the Group on several occasions, finishing up by leading the Battle of Britain Fly Past over London with many squadrons of bombers and fighters following. This was a day of very poor visibility due to fog, and the 12.30 hrs time over Big Ben had to be postponed to 16.30 hrs, when we went over on the dot, to my intense relief. I did fly for three more months before my retirement, but I look on this great occasion as my personal swan song.

When I landed at Northolt—by special arrangement as it was then being used as London Airport while Heathrow was being constructed—I was embarrassingly given a tremendous reception, with requests for autographs, etc. The loudspeakers had apparently handed out some glowing details while I was landing, as the Leader of the Fly Past and I don't know what else! I was able to get away in my car which had come to collect me, and so, soon, I left my wonderful Group and the Royal Air Force after just thirty-five thrilling years.

These years must for ever be the best time for anyone to have served in our Service. The aircraft having changed so dramatically in that period from box kites to jets—Maurice

Farman Longhorn to Meteor: armament, in my case, from a single slow unreliable Lewis gun to 20 and 40 mm cannons and homing rockets; bombs from hand-held 20 lb Coopers to 4,000 and even 10,000 lb monsters, electronically aimed through cloud—and then nuclear weapons.

The addition of parachutes, wireless telegraphy to radio telephony and radar navigational aids (instead of reading the name of a railway station to find out where you were!)

At the beginning of my time, if flying across country, the rule was always to have a field chosen in which one could land in the event of an expected failure. As that field was passed, a new one had to be selected. Always look for smoke or which way the cattle are facing when feeding, to show the direction of the wind. Look for grass, rather than crops which wound round the axle and turned a machine over on its back. Having looked for the railway station's name—when lost—climb up over it to a safe height and try to find 'BOVRIL' on the map!

Actually, I have never lost touch . . . never having recovered from my flying fever. I go to various Service aerodromes, noting with amazement and appreciation the wonderful advances made and the truly professional ability of pilots and ground crews compared with the times when I learnt on the old Maurice Farman. I find often that I'd very much like to jump aboard a modern aeroplane when no one's looking and try my luck! What a headline! 'Air Vice-Marshal hi-jacks plane'!

I think I can truly say I am not envious, as I consider my thirty-five years of advancement were the most interesting that could be and I am very certain that we had more 'fun'.

I did fly a very interesting assortment of aeroplanes, consisting of: monoplane, biplane, triplane, tractor, pusher, rotary engined, radial engined, stationary engined, jet engined, single engined, twin engined, glider—a total of over 120 distinct different types.

'Old men forget', they say, but they remember too, and in jotting down this rough account of what I remember, I have relived the past, and, what is more, broken what for me is new ground . . . a trial flight! Nor am I the only one to remember, as my button-hook proves!

For, indeed, among my souvenirs, I value very highly a button-hook made from various pieces of metal from my Avro in which I crashed at Gosport in 1917. Let a few extracts from the letter—received in August 1971 while this last chapter was being written—which accompanied it, speak for itself:

'I think I had better introduce myself; you were my Flight Commander in "B" Flight at the School of Special Flying, Fort Grange . . . You had some very hectic moments during the war and it is very good to know you came home safe and sound after a brilliant and sound Air Force career . . . I never thought you would ever have flown again after your air crash in 1917. I am sending you a little thing I made out of the machine in which you had your accident; it is composed of different materials off the machine. I have had it 53 years and it has been with me on various aerodromes in Canada. As I say again, I am a very proud man to know that I served under you.'

It would be idle to pretend that this object has been of great practical use to me: I rather fancy I abandoned spats in the early 20s or thereabouts! But as somebody said: 'It's the thought that matters', and that gave me great pleasure. And that, come to think of it, is not a bad thought with which to end the story of my flying fever.

Index

compiled by Bruce Robertson